THE BEST OF
SAINSBURY'S

ITALIAN
COOKING

THE BEST OF
SAINSBURY'S
ITALIAN
COOKING

CONTENTS

CONTRIBUTORS

Main author: Carole Handslip

Contributing authors: Michelle Berriedale Johnson, Carol Bowen, Gill Edden, Caroline Ellwood, Claire Ferguson, Wendy Godfrey, Claire Gordon Smith, Heather Lambert, Norma MacMillan, Rhona Newman, Mary Reynolds, Julia Roles and Sue Ross.

Special Photography: David Gill

NOTES

Standard spoon measures are used in all recipes
1 tablespoon = one 15 ml spoon
1 teaspoon = one 5 ml spoon
All spoon measures are level.

Size 3 eggs should be used unless otherwise stated.

Ovens should be preheated to the specified temperature.

For all the recipes, quantities are given in both metric and imperial measures. Follow either set but not a mixture of both because they are not interchangeable.

If fresh yeast is unobtainable, substitute dried yeast but use only half the recommended quantity and follow the manufacturer's instructions for reconstituting.

Fresh herbs are used unless otherwise stated. If unobtainable substitute a bouquet garni of the equivalent dried herbs or use dried herbs instead but halve the quantities stated.

Published exclusively for
J Sainsbury plc
Stamford House
Stamford Street,
London SE1 9LL
by Reed International Books Limited
Michelin House
81 Fulham Road
London SW3 6RB

First published in Great Britain in 1992

© Reed International Books Limited 1992

ISBN 0-600-57693-0

Produced by Mandarin Offset
Printed and Bound in Hong Kong

INTRODUCTION

Italian food has been described as being 'the mother of all European Latin cuisines' – it is therefore hardly surprising to find that today its popularity is still strong. In fact it could be said that with today's busy schedules, demands for fast food, yet desire for healthy Italian food recipes is more popular than ever. The clever way in which the Italians conjure up simple and uncomplicated food, using fresh foods in season, employing basic cooking methods, yet very cleverly combining foods with just the right seasoning, ensures its longevity for many more years to come.

It isn't difficult to become a devotee of Italian cuisine when you consider that you can feast on antipasti, soups, rice and pasta dishes, poultry and game specialities, fresh fish and seafood, meat in many guises, pizzas and special breads, baked treats and desserts. Whether you are entertaining or simply cooking for family or friends you will find recipes suitable for every occasion. You could choose a delicious colourful pasta or fish dish from Southern Italy; or a sophisticated meat or poultry dish from Tuscany.

The Italians use a wide range of herbs, cheeses, preserved meats, pasta, seasonings and oils in their recipes – the introduction that follows will give you guidelines on how to use them for dramatic and authentic effect. A dash of olive oil, sprinkling of freshly-grated Parmesan or Pecorino cheese or teaspoonful or two of chopped fresh basil in just the right proportions at the right time will markedly improve a recipe and give a wonderful taste of Italy.

ITALIAN COOKING

REGIONAL COOKING

Until 1861 Italy was a collection of independent states, each with its own laws, customs and traditions. Today, as you travel from one area to another, you will notice regional differences between the landscape, people, dialects and foods.

There is a particularly marked difference between northern and southern Italy: regions in the north tend to be more industrial and prosperous than those in the poorer south and the northern soil tends to be more fertile. The differences as far as cooking is concerned are that the traditional northern pasta is the flat variety, freshly made with eggs; the fat used for cooking is generally butter. In the south, tubular varieties of pasta are more common and olive oil is used for cooking. Flavours are much stronger in the south because of the extensive use of herbs and aromatics, particularly in sauces.

Well-known pasta dishes of the northern province of Liguria include ravioli and tortellini. The rice-growing area in the Po Valley, just behind Venice, provides abundant supplies of arborio rice. This especially absorbent medium-grained rice is the basis for risottos and an excellent way of making small amounts of meat or shellfish stretch to feed a large family. Many delicious risotto recipes have evolved, some of which are included in this book.

Two of the most famous products of the north are Parmesan cheese and Parma ham, both from Parma. Parmesan cheese is at its best after 2 years of drying and maturing, and becomes stronger the longer it is left. The whey from the cheese is fed to the Parma pigs and, combined with the careful salting and drying processes on the hillsides, results in the delicately flavoured ham.

Italy is virtually surrounded by sea and locally caught fish are a dominant feature of most regional cuisines. Venice is particularly noted for its red and grey mullet, squid, scampi and mussels. In the north, seafish supplies are supplemented by excellent freshwater fish from the Lakes of Lombardy – especially eels. The southern coast and the islands of Sicily and Sardinia are dotted with fishing villages. Here, tuna, sardines, swordfish and a variety of shellfish are caught and used locally in pasta dishes, sauces, soups, stews and salads.

Abundant local supplies of tomatoes, garlic, herbs and anchovies in the southern regions give dishes their characteristic aromatic quality. Naples, the culinary centre of the south, claims the invention of the pizza and ice cream as we know it today. Pizzas are baked in open-brick ovens of pizzerias and bakeries, and most often eaten as snacks. Mozzarella, the cheese used for pizza toppings, has been made for centuries in the surrounding countryside of Campania. It is an ideal 'melting' cheese and lends itself to all types of pizzas and cooked dishes. The equally famous Italian ices are made in mouth-watering flavours and, like the pizza, have spread all over Italy and further afield.

Italy is the world's largest wine producer and almost every region makes its contribution to the great variety of exported table wines. Piemonte is the home of Barolo, a fine red to accompany roast meat and game, and the modest but flavoursome Barbera, an ideal wine to drink with robust pasta dishes and pizzas. Veneto provides two popular wines: the dry, red Valpolicella and Soave – a medium white wine. From Tuscany comes the deservedly famous Chianti Classico, the perfect accompaniment to roasts, grills and game dishes. Other Italian wines worth trying are Orvieto, Verdicchio, Frascati and Lambrusco.

SPECIALIST INGREDIENTS

Delicatessens and good supermarkets offer an ever-increasing number of Italian ingredients. Most items can be obtained from these or a simple substitute can be used.

CHEESES

Parmesan: Unique cheese, grated and added to sauces, pasta, rice and other dishes to give an incomparable flavour. It is best bought by the piece; ready-grated Parmesan is good but cannot compare with the freshly-grated cheese.

Mozzarella: A white cheese, used extensively in cooking for its melting properties, especially as a topping for pizzas. It is sold in small packets and, when very fresh, is moist and dripping with whey. Bel Paese can be used as a substitute.

Ricotta: A soft, white cheese, made from whey. Must be eaten absolutely fresh. Used in savoury stuffings and sweet fillings. Medium fat curd cheese makes a good substitute.

Gorgonzola: The famous Italian blue-veined table cheese. When ripe, it should be mild and soft.

Other Italian table cheeses to look out for are Bel Paese, Boscailo Taleggio and Provolone.

CURED MEATS AND SAUSAGES

Bresaola: Dry cured beef fillet, eaten raw in wafer thin slices. A highly esteemed antipasto.

Parma: Delicately cured ham, eaten raw and wafer thin. No real substitute, but for cooked dishes use smoked ham.

Salami: Long dry-cured sausages of lean ground meat with pork fat and spices. There are various types, of which Salami Milano is considered the best. Serve sliced in mixed antipasti, chopped in stuffings.

Mortadella: Large smooth-textured cooked pork sausage laced with pork fat and spices. Serve sliced for antipasti, chopped in stuffings.

Cotechino: Lightly cured pork sausage, weighing from 500g to 1 kg (1 to 2 lb). It is first boiled, then thickly sliced and served with lentils or beans, or cold with salad.

Luganega: Long, thin coiled sausage of mild, coarsely ground pork. Also called *Salsiccia*. Fry, grill or boil and serve hot with lentils or potatoes. Any fresh sausage with a high meat content can be used as a substitute.

HERBS

Herbs are an essential flavouring in many Italian dishes. Fresh herbs are normally used in Italy; fortunately these are becoming increasingly available in shops. However, it is well worth growing a selection of herbs in pots on the window or in the garden. Use dried herbs when fresh ones are unavailable, but replace regularly to avoid staleness.

The following herbs are the ones most commonly used in Italian cooking.

Basil: The incomparable herb for tomato dishes. Also popular in salads, sauces and soups.

Bay Leaves: As a flavouring for casseroles, soups and roasts; also put onto the fire at barbecues for aroma.

Oregano: Common ingredient in many dishes, especially pizzas, casseroles and sauces.

Parsley: The universal herb for flavouring Italian savoury dishes. Italian parsley is the flat-leaved variety so use this when available.

Rosemary: Strongly-flavoured herb, used mainly for roast lamb or pork. Also chicken and fish dishes.

Sage: Especially for flavouring veal and chicken dishes cooked in wine.

STORECUPBOARD INGREDIENTS

The following non-perishable ingredients are frequently used in Italian dishes and it is useful to keep a stock of them.

Rice: Italian risotto rice is thicker, shorter and absorbs more liquid than other types of rice. It is essential for a creamy risotto. Italian long-grain rice is sold in an 'easy cook' form.

Beans: Dried haricot beans and lentils, canned white cannellini and pink/brown borlotti beans are used for soups, salads and other dishes.

Pepper and Salt: Italians always use freshly ground black peppercorns from a pepper mill and, whenever possible, coarse sea salt.

Wine Vinegar: Essential for salad dressings and used in many other recipes.

Olive and Vegetable Oils: The distinctive flavour of good olive oil is needed for salad dressings and for cooking where olive oil gives the dish a special character. Otherwise groundnut or sunflower oil are suitable.

Anchovy Fillets in oil: For adding zest to sauces, pizzas and antipasti dishes.

Capers: Small capers add authenticity to various sauces, fish dishes and garnishes.

Olives: Keep small bottles or cans of green, black and stuffed olives, but buy fresh loose ones when possible.

Canned Tomatoes: These 'plum' tomatoes have an excellent flavour and are time-saving and convenient for all sauces and casseroles. Use them for cooking in preference to fresh tomatoes.

Tomato Purée: Small amounts are invaluable for strengthening the flavour and colour of dishes in which fresh or canned tomatoes are used.

Fortified Wines: Dry white Vermouth can be used in recipes needing white wine and herbs; it is stronger than table wine so less is needed. Medium Marsala gives a richness to veal, poultry and ham dishes.

PASTA

Pasta is a good source of carbohydrate and the wholewheat variety has a higher fibre content. If you are counting calories, reduce the amount of butter and oil used in the recipes and choose a sauce, which is low in calories.

As well as the many dried varieties of pasta available, an increasing number of stores now sell fresh pasta which is very near the flavour and texture of home-made pasta.

Anyone who is adept at pastry-making will have no trouble in making their own pasta. It may take a few practice runs, but it is well worth the trouble. Don't give up after the first attempt – practice really does make perfect. Home-made pasta has an individual flavour which will certainly be appreciated.

Most of the recipes in this book use fresh pasta, which can be the bought variety or your own home-made if time allows. Allow about 125 g (4 oz) fresh pasta per person for a main course, depending on how substantial the sauce is and the size of the appetite, and about 50 g (2 oz) for a starter. If

dried pasta is used, it is specified in the recipe. If you choose to use a dried variety instead of fresh, allow 75-125 g (3-4 oz) dried pasta per person for a main course, and 50-75 g (2-3 oz) for a starter.

The pasta dough on page 150 can be used to make all types of pasta. It is referred to in the recipes as '500 g (1 lb) quantity pasta dough', where it is intended home-made dough should be used, although you may buy ready-made pasta shapes if preferred. If you use the dough recipe to make your own tagliatelle, etc, either adjust the basic recipe to give you the amount specified, or make it all up and freeze any leftover pasta for up to 3 months.

Cooking Pasta

All pasta must be cooked in plenty of boiling water. As a guide, allow at least 4 litres (7 pints) water for 500 g (1 lb) pasta. *Never use less than 3 litres (5¼ pints) even for a small amount.* Do not attempt to cook more than 1 kg (2 lb) in one pan, as it is difficult to stir, season and drain. The addition of oil prevents the pasta pieces from sticking together.

Bring the water, 1-2 tablespoons oil and 1-2 teaspoons salt to the boil. Add the pasta and return to the boil.

Cook uncovered, stirring occasionally, until *al dente* – just tender but firm to the bite. For fresh pasta this will take about 3 to 4 minutes (10 to 15 minutes for filled types); dried pasta will take about 9 to 12 minutes. With dried pasta follow the cooking times on the packet or the recipe – test the pasta frequently during cooking. Pasta that is over-cooked and soft is unappetizing.

As soon as it is *al dente*, drain the pasta to stop it softening further, toss in butter and coat in sauce to prevent it drying out. Serve immediately, accompanied by freshly-grated Parmesan.

Types of Pasta

The varieties of pasta are endless. Freshly-made tagliatelle, paglia e fieno and spaghetti are available in good supermarkets and delicatessens, as well as some stuffed varieties such as tortellini and cappelletti.

There is an excellent range of dried pasta in most stores. A selection of the many varieties available is illustrated opposite. For those of us in a hurry, there is an excellent dried lasagne and cannelloni on the market which requires no pre-cooking. Follow the instructions on the packet.

DRIED PASTA VARIETIES

1. Fusilli
2. Tortellini
3. Farfalle
4. Conchiglie
5. Wholewheat macaroni
6. Fusilli
7. Pasta spirals
8. Tagliatelle verdi
9. Tagliatelle
10. Wholewheat tagliatelle
11. Rigatoni
12. Conchigliette piccole
13. Wholewheat spaghetti
14. Pasta wheels
15. Spaghetti
16. Vermicelli
17. Lasagne verdi
18. Lasagne
19. Wholewheat rigatoni
20. Penne

SOUPS AND STARTERS

Few visitors to Italy can resist the tempting display of antipasti (hors d'oeuvre or starters) found on most lunch and dinner-time menus. Many include a collection of small dishes of cured meats, dressed shellfish, olives, raw vegetables and piquant, tasty salads designed to be served together like fried seafood, Parma ham with figs, artichokes in vinaigrette, mussels in a spicy sauce or eggs with a piquant mayonnaise; while others may include a restaurant or regional speciality intended to be savoured separately.

The recipes in this section have been chosen so that you can make your own mixed Italian-style antipasti start to a meal or enjoy a regional speciality like Sicilian Sweet-Sour Vegetables (page 29). Not forgetting that arranged attractively and chosen judiciously a good antipasti will also make an excellent light lunch or supper dish as well as a starter to a main meal.

The soups featured also represent the vast choice open to the Italian housewife, so fish soups line up with pasta, country vegetable and garlic-based soups. Arranged alongside all-time pasta and rice favourites like risotto, cannelloni, ravioli and spaghetti, made with tasty fillings and sauces, there is a veritable feast of ideas to start a meal.

'RAGGED' EGG SOUP

2 eggs
2 tablespoons fine
    semolina
50 g (2 oz) grated
    Parmesan cheese
1.2 litres (2 pints)
    Chicken Broth (see
    this page)

Beat together the eggs, semolina, cheese and about 200 ml (7 fl oz) chicken broth. Heat the remaining broth until almost boiling, immediately remove from the heat and beat in the egg mixture.

Continue beating over a low heat for 2 to 3 minutes, just until the eggs break into 'ragged' flakes. Serve immediately.
Serves 4 to 6

CHICKEN BROTH

This forms the basis of many soups. The chicken can be served hot for the main course, or cold with Piquant Green Sauce or Tuna Fish Mayonnaise (see page 152).

1 × 1.5 kg (3½ lb)
    oven-ready chicken
1.2 litres (2 pints)
    water
1 carrot, sliced
1 onion, sliced
2 celery sticks, sliced
2 tomatoes, quartered
1 bay leaf
6 peppercorns
1 teaspoon salt
1 chicken stock cube
    (optional)

Put the prepared chicken into a deep pan and add the water. Bring slowly to the boil and remove any scum. Add the vegetables, bay leaf, peppercorns and salt. Cover and simmer very gently until the chicken is tender, about 1 hour. Lift out the chicken. Strain the broth and check the seasoning; if necessary, crumble in the stock cube and stir until dissolved.
Makes about 1.2 litres (2 pints)

'Ragged' Egg Soup; Chicken Broth

RAVIOLI

DOUGH:
250 g (8 oz) strong
   plain flour
good pinch of salt
50 g (2 oz) butter,
   softened
little boiling water to
   mix

FILLING:
125 g (4 oz) grated
   Parmesan cheese
175 g (6 oz) Gruyère
   cheese, grated
3 eggs, beaten
1 teaspoon grated
   nutmeg
1 teaspoon each
   chopped basil and
   marjoram
salt and pepper
little milk to mix (if
   necessary)

TO SERVE:
grated Parmesan
   cheese
chopped herbs

Sift the flour and salt into a bowl. Rub in the butter until the mixture resembles breadcrumbs. Add sufficient boiling water to give a pliable but firm dough. Turn onto a floured surface and knead well. Divide the dough in half, wrap in clingfilm and set aside.

Mix together the cheeses, eggs, nutmeg, herbs, and salt and pepper to taste to give a firm mixture, adding a little milk if it is too stiff.

Roll out both pieces of dough on a floured surface until paper thin.

Place teaspoonfuls of the cheese and herb mixture on one piece of dough at 4 cm (1½ inch) intervals. Cover with the second sheet of pasta, without stretching it. Lightly press down around the mounds of filling. Using a pastry wheel, separate each ravioli, making sure the edges are sealed. Leave to dry for 2 to 3 hours.

Cook in boiling salted water for 4 to 5 minutes. Drain and serve with plenty of Parmesan and herbs.
Serves 6

Ravioli

POOR MAN'S SOUP

4 slices of Italian
   bread
1 large clove garlic,
   peeled
750 g (1½ lb)
   broccoli spears
1.2 litres (2 pints)
   chicken stock
salt and pepper
125 g (4 oz) grated
   Parmesan cheese

Toast the bread until golden, allow to cool then rub with the garlic to flavour.

Cook the broccoli in a pan of boiling salted water until just tender, about 5-6 minutes. Drain and cut into bit-sized pieces.

Bring the stock slowly to the boil. Place a piece of bread in the bottom of four soup plates. Top with an equal quantity of the broccoli pieces. Season with salt and pepper to taste and sprinkle with the Parmesan cheese. Carefully ladle the stock over the toast and serve at once.
Serves 4

CHILLED FISH SOUP

500 g (1 lb) shell-on
   cooked prawns
2 strips lemon peel
2 bay leaves
900 ml (1½ pints)
   water
salt and pepper
4 small squid,
   cleaned, gutted and
   cut into thin rings
3 tomatoes, skinned,
   seeded and chopped
2 teaspoons snipped
   chives

Peel the prawns, reserving the shells and heads. Place the shells and heads in a pan with the lemon peel, bay leaves, water and salt and pepper to taste. Bring to the boil, reduce the heat, cover and simmer for 30 minutes. Strain well and discard the prawn shells, heads, lemon peel and bay leaves.

Return the stock to the pan, add the squid and cook for 5 minutes. Remove from the heat and allow to cool.

When cool, stir in the prawns, tomatoes and chives. Cover and chill for at least 1 hour before serving.
Serves 4

Mackerel Mushrooms

MACKEREL MUSHROOMS

250 (8 oz) button
  mushrooms, thinly
  sliced
2 smoked mackerel
  fillets, skinned and
  chopped
DRESSING:
5 tablespoons olive
  oil
1 teaspoon lemon
  juice
2 tablespoons red
  wine vinegar
pinch chilli powder
salt and pepper
GARNISH:
2 teaspoons chopped
  parsley

Place all the dressing ingredients in a screw-top jar, seasoning to taste with a little chilli powder and with salt and pepper.

Place the mushrooms in a shallow bowl, add the chopped mackerel and pour over the dressing. Mix well, and leave in a cool place, but not the refrigerator, for about 30 minutes.

Transfer the salad to a serving dish, sprinkle on the parsley and toss to mix well.

Serves 4

NOTE: In place of the mackerel you could, if you wished, use 50g (2 oz) can anchovies, drained and sliced.

PARMA ROULADE

250 g (8 oz) Parma
  or other smoked
  ham
250 g (8 oz) cream
  cheese
2-3 parsley sprigs,
  chopped
peppe

Trim the slices of ham to neat rectangles. Place the ham trimmings in a processor and chop finely. Add the cream cheese and parsley and blend well. Season with pepper to taste.

Roll into sausage shapes as long as the width of the ham slices. Place a cheese roll at one end of each ham slice and roll up. Cover and chill for 2 hours.

Serve accompanied by slices of melon, pear or figs.

Serves 4

MINESTRONE

175 g (6 oz) cabbage
1 large onion
2 large carrot
2 celery sticks
2 courgettes
3 tomatoes, skinned
50 g (2 oz) streaky
  bacon, derinded
2 tablespoons oil
2 cloves garlic,
  crushed
1.75 litres (3 pints)
  water
4 sage or basil leaves,
  chopped
75 g (3 oz) long-
  grain rice
2 tablespoons
  chopped parsley
2 tablespoons grated
  Parmesan cheese
salt and pepper

Shred the cabbage; chop the other vegetables and the bacon. Heat the oil in a large saucepan, add the bacon, onion, carrot, celery and garlic and fry gently, stirring frequently, for about 10 minutes.

Add the water, bring to the boil and add the cabbage, courgettes, tomatoes, sage or basil, and rice. Continue cooking gently for 20 minutes.

Stir in the parsley, cheese, and salt and pepper to taste.

Serve with extra Parmesan cheese and crusty bread.

Serves 6

NOTE: Small pasta (pastina) may be used instead of rice.

HEARTY FISH SOUP

2 tablespoons oil
1 large onion,
    chopped
1 clove garlic, crushed
3 celery sticks, diced
2 × 397 g (14 oz)
    can of chopped
    tomatoes
900 ml (1½ pints)
    fish or chicken
    stock
¼ teaspoon dried
    oregano
¼ teaspoon dried
    basil
¼ teaspoon dried
    rosemary
65 g (2½ oz) long-
    grain rice
250 g (8 oz) sliced
    green beans
750 g (1½ lb) cod or
    halibut fillets,
    cubed.
salt and pepper
2 tablespoons
    chopped parsley

Heat the oil in a saucepan. Add the onion, garlic and celery and fry until softened. Stir in the tomatoes with their juice, stock, herbs and rice. Bring to the boil, then cover and simmer for 10 minutes.

Add the beans and continue simmering, covered, until the rice is tender. Add the fish and simmer for 5 minutes or until the fish is tender. Adjust the seasoning and sprinkle with parsley.

Serves 6 to 8

MIXED FRIED FISH

4 squid
6 extra large prawns,
    peeled
2 fillets plaice or sole,
    cut into 5 cm (2
    inch) strips
oil for deep-frying
BATTER:
125 g (4 oz) plain
    flour
pinch of salt
2 tablespoons olive
    oil
150 ml (¼ pint)
    water
1 large egg white
    (size 1), stiffly
    whisked
TO GARNISH:
lemon slices
fried parsley

Prepare the squid as described below. Place in a pan of boiling water and cook for 2 minutes. Drain and dry on kitchen paper. Set aside with the prawns and the plaice or sole.

To make the batter, sift the flour and salt into a bowl, gradually add the oil and water, then fold in the egg white.

Heat the oil in a deep-fryer to 190°C (375°F). Dip each type of fish in turn into the batter, drain off any excess, then fry in the hot oil until golden brown. Drain on kitchen paper and keep hot while frying the remaining fish.

Arrange the fried fish on a warmed serving dish. Garnish with lemon slices and fried parsley.

Serves 6

FETTUCCINE WITH MUSHROOMS

500 g (1 lb) dried
    fettuccine
salt and pepper
50 g (2 oz) butter
1 tablespoon olive oil
1 clove garlic, crushed
175 g (6 oz) button
    mushrooms, sliced
142 ml (¼ pint)
    carton double
    cream
grated Parmesan
    cheese to serve

Cook the fettuccine in boiling salted water according to the packet instructions until just tender.

Meanwhile, melt the butter and oil in a pan, add the garlic and cook for 1 minute, without browning. Add the mushrooms and fry for 2 minutes. Add the cream and simmer for 10 minutes stirring occasionally. Season with salt and pepper to taste. Remove from the heat and leave for 2 minutes.

Drain the pasta and add to the sauce; toss well.

Serve immediately, with Parmesan cheese.

Serves 6

PREPARING SQUID

To prepare squid, begin by removing the head from the body sac. Cut off the lower part of the head and remove the polyp in the centre, leaving only the tentacles. Wash the sac in cold, running water and remove the transparent fin from the inside. Pull away the outer skin of the sac. Cut the sac into rings, about 6 mm (¼ inch) wide, and cut the tentacles into slices.

MINTED MELON WITH PROSCIUTTO

1 small head radicchio
2 Cantaloupe melons
125 g (4 oz) Parma
  ham, cut into strips
DRESSING:
3 tablespoons lemon
  juice
4 fresh sprigs mint
150 g (5 oz) thick set
  natural yogurt
1 teaspoon chopped
  parsley
1 teaspoon snipped
  chives
salt and pepper

Divide and wash the radicchio leaves, tearing any large leaves into smaller pieces and arrange on four individual serving plates.

Halve the melons, scoop out the seeds then remove the flesh with a melon baller or small spoon. Mix with the ham and spoon over the radicchio.

To make the dressing, place the lemon juice in a bowl, add the mint and crush with a fork to bruise the leaves. Leave to stand for 10 minutes then remove and discard the mint. Add the yogurt, parsley, chives and salt and pepper to taste. Spoon over the melon and ham mixture and serve at once.
Serves 4

AVOCADO WITH TOMATO DRESSING

4 tablespoons Passata
3 tablespoons
  mayonnaise
1 tablespoon chopped
  capers
1 teaspoon snipped
  chives
salt and pepper
2 avocados

To make the dressing, mix the Passata with the mayonnaise until smooth. Stir in the capers, chives and salt and pepper to taste.

Peel, halve and stone the avocados then cut into thin slices. Arrange on four individual serving plates. Spoon over the prepared tomato dressing and serve at once.
Serves 4

Mediterranean Cheese Mould

FUSILLI WITH LEEK AND HAM

250 g (8 oz) dried
    fusilli
50 g (2 oz) butter
1 large leek, very
    finely shredded
1 small onion, finely
    chopped
5 tablespoons single
    cream
75 g (3 oz) Parma
    ham, cut into small
    pieces
50 g (2 oz) Parmesan
    cheese, grated
salt and pepper

Cook the pasta in boiling salted water, according to the packet instructions until just tender. Drain and place in a heated serving bowl.

Meanwhile, melt the butter in a pan, add the leek and onion and cook gently until just softened.

Add the cream, ham, leek mixture, Parmesan and salt and pepper to taste to the pasta and toss gently to mix. Serve at once.
Serves 4

MEDITERRANEAN CHEESE MOULD

250 g (8 oz) cottage
    cheese
2 teaspoons finely
    chopped onion
2 tomatoes, skinned,
    seeded and finely
    chopped
1 tablespoon anchovy
    fish paste
few drops of anchovy
    essence (optional)
salt and pepper
TO GARNISH:
shredded lettuce
parsley sprigs
tomato slices

Place the cottage cheese in a bowl and add the onion, tomatoes, anchovy paste and essence, if using. Blend well and add salt and pepper to taste. Press into a 250 g (8 oz) serving dish or mould. Chill in the refrigerator for 2 to 3 hours. Turn out onto a serving dish and surround with lettuce. Garnish with parsley and tomato. Serve with rye bread, toast or crispbreads.
Serves 4
VARIATIONS:
1. Omit the tomatoes, anchovy paste and essence and add 1 teaspoon made mustard and two teaspoons finely chopped walnuts.
2. Replace the anchovy paste and essence with 2 teaspoons each chopped parsley, chives and thyme.

ALMOND ROULADE

3 eggs, separated
25 g (1 oz) light soft
    brown sugar
1/2 teaspoon salt
125 g (4 oz) ground
    almonds
FILLING:
125 g (4 oz) peeled
    prawns
300 ml (1/2 pint)
    mayonnaise
1 tablespoon chopped
    parsley
1 tablespoon chopped
    capers
1 tablespoon chopped
    gherkins
salt and pepper
TO GARNISH:
shredded lettuce

Put the egg yolks in a warm bowl and whisk for 5 minutes. Add the sugar and salt and whisk for 7 minutes. Whisk the egg whites until stiff, then fold into the egg yolk mixture. Finally fold in the almonds.

Turn into a 30 × 20 cm (12 × 8 inch) Swiss roll tin lined with greaseproof paper, spreading the mixture into the corners. Bake in a preheated moderate oven, 180°C (350°F), Gas Mark 4, for 12 to 15 minutes, until firm and lightly browned. Turn out onto a sheet of greaseproof paper and carefully remove the paper. Leave until cold.

Mix all the filling ingredients together, adding salt and pepper to taste.

When the roulade is cold, spread with the filling and roll up like a Swiss roll. Serve garnished with shredded lettuce.
Serves 6

Almond Roulade

TORTELLINI BOLOGNESE

25 g (1 oz) butter
125 g (4 oz) lean
    pork, chopped
75 g (3 oz) lean veal,
    chopped
1 small chicken
    breast, chopped
50 g (2 oz) cooked
    ham, chopped
25 g (1 oz)
    Mortadella,
    chopped
salt and pepper
75 g (3 oz) Parmesan
    cheese, grated
2 eggs
½ teaspoon grated
    nutmeg
500 g (1 lb) plain
    flour
pinch of salt
3 eggs
cold water to mix
melted butter and
    grated Parmesan
    cheese to serve

Melt the butter in a pan, add the pork, veal and chicken and brown lightly. Add the ham, Mortadella, and salt and pepper to taste. Cover and cook for 15 minutes. Cool slightly, then mince the meat. Mix in the Parmesan, eggs and nutmeg.

Sift the flour and salt onto a board, make a hollow in the centre and add the eggs. Work to a stiff dough, adding a little water if necessary. With floured hands, knead until smooth. Roll out on a floured surface until paper thin. Using a 4 cm (1½ inch) fluted cutter, cut into rounds.

Spoon a little filling onto each round, dampen the edges, then fold to form semi-circles. Curl them, bringing the two points together. Place on a floured tray, cover with a cloth and leave to dry for 12 hours.

Cook in boiling salted water for 5 to 7 minutes; drain. Toss in melted butter and sprinkle liberally with grated Parmesan cheese to serve.
Serves 6 to 8

PRAWN AND MUSHROOM RISOTTO

1 tablespoon olive oil
15 g (½ oz) butter
2 cloves garlic,
    crushed
1 onion, sliced
50 g (2 oz)
    mushrooms, sliced
175 g (6 oz) Italian
    risotto rice
2 tablespoons lemon
    juice
2 tablespoons parsley
salt and pepper
150 ml (¼ pint) hot
    fish or vegetable
    stock
150 ml (¼ pint)
    Italian dry white
    wine
375 g (12 oz) peeled
    prawns

Heat the oil with the butter in a large, heavy-based frying pan. Add the garlic and onion and fry until golden brown. Add the mushrooms and rice and cook for 1 minute, stirring constantly.

Add the lemon juice, parsley, salt and pepper to taste, stock and wine. Bring to the boil, reduce the heat and cook, uncovered, for 12-15 minutes until the rice is almost cooked and just a little liquid remains.

Add the prawns, mixing well and cook for a further 3-5 minutes or until the rice is cooked, the prawns are heated through and no excess liquid remains. Serve at once.
Serves 4

RUSTICA PIE

PASTRY:
250 g (8 oz) plain
  flour
pinch of salt
175 g (6 oz) butter
squeeze of lemon
  juice
little iced water to
  mix
FILLING:
3 eggs, beaten
375 g (12 oz) Ricotta
  or cottage cheese
125 g (4 oz)
  Parmesan cheese,
  grated
1 onion, chopped
2 tablespoons
  chopped chives
salt and pepper
1 tablespoon oil
2 cloves garlic,
  crushed
375 g (12 oz)
  tomatoes, skinned,
  seeded and chopped
4 tablespoons tomato
  purée
4 tablespoons dry
  white wine
1/2 teaspoon each
  dried marjoram
  and oregano
125 g (4 oz) black
  olives, pitted
250 g (8 oz)
  Mozzarella
  cheese, sliced
1 green pepper,
  cored, seeded and
  thinly sliced

Sift the flour and salt into a bowl and rub in the butter until the mixture resembles fine breadcrumbs. Add the lemon juice and enough water to give a firm dough. Cover and chill for 30 minutes.

Meanwhile, prepare the filling. Mix together the eggs, cheeses, onion and chives. Season well with salt and pepper.

Heat the oil in a pan, add the garlic and cook for 1 minute, without browning. Stir in the tomatoes, tomato purée, wine, herbs and salt and pepper to taste. Bring to the boil and cook rapidly for about 15 minutes, until thickened; cool.

Divide the pastry in half. Roll out one piece and use to line a 23 cm (9 inch) pie dish. Roll out the other piece for a lid.

Spread half the cheese mixture over the base. Sprinkle over half the olives and arrange half the cheese slices on top. Spoon over half the tomato sauce and arrange half the pepper slices on top. Repeat the layers and cover with the pastry lid. Seal and flute the edges and make 3 or 4 diagonal slashes through the lid.

Bake in a preheated hot oven, 220°C (425°F), Gas Mark 7, for 35 minutes, until golden brown.

Leave for 30 minutes before serving.
Serves 6 to 8

FISHERMAN'S SALAD

4 squid
4–6 shelled scallops,
  quartered
18 mussels in shells,
  scrubbed clean
375 g (12 oz) peeled
  prawns
1 × 170 g (6 oz) can
  crabmeat, drained
6 tablespoons olive
  oil
3 tablespoons lemon
  juice
1 clove garlic, crushed
2 tablespoons
  chopped parsley
1 tablespoon chopped
  fennel (optional)
salt and pepper
lemon slices to
  garnish

To prepare squid, see the instructions on page 15.

Cook the scallops in a pan containing 300 ml (1/2 pint) boiling water for 2 to 3 minutes. Remove with a slotted spoon and set aside.

Add the squid to the pan and cook for 15 minutes, until tender. Remove with a slotted spoon and set aside.

Add the mussels to the pan and cook for about 5 minutes until the shells have opened; discard any that do not. Drain and remove the top shell from each mussel.

Put all the shellfish into a bowl. Mix the oil, lemon juice, garlic and herbs together, adding salt and pepper to taste. Pour over the fish and toss well. Cover and chill for 30 minutes.

Garnish with lemon slices and serve with brown bread.
Serves 6

LEFT: *Tortellini Bolognese*

RIGHT: *Fisherman's Salad*

COLD CUCUMBER SOUP

1 large cucumber
3 × 150 g (5 oz)
  cartons natural
  low-fat yogurt
142 ml (¼ pint)
  carton of soured
  cream
salt and pepper
1-2 tablespoons finely
  chopped mint
mint sprigs to garnish

Peel the cucumber and grate coarsely. Mix with the yogurt, soured cream, and salt and pepper to taste. Chill for about 2 hours

Stir in chopped mint to taste. Pour into chilled soup bowls and top with mint sprigs to garnish.
Serves 6

VENETIAN BAKED ARTICHOKES

400 g (13 oz) can
  artichoke bottoms
  or prepared and
  cooked fresh
  bottoms
2 hard-boiled
  eggs, shelled
50 g (2 oz) smoked
  ham
2 teaspoons chopped
  fresh basil
2 tablespoons
  chopped parsley
salt and pepper
75 g (3 oz) fresh
  breadcrumbs
olive oil to sprinkle

Drain the canned artichoke bottoms thoroughly. Alternatively, remove the bases from fresh artichokes and cook until tender in boiling, salted water, about 10 minutes then drain thoroughly.

Finely chop the eggs and ham and mix with the basil, parsley and salt and pepper to taste. Use this mixture to stuff the artichoke bases then place in a greased ovenproof dish. Sprinkle with the breadcrumbs and drizzle with just enough olive oil to moisten.

Bake in a preheated moderate oven, 180°C (350°F), Gas Mark 4, for about 15-20 minutes until golden. Serve hot or cold.
Serves 4

TAGLIATELLE WITH PRAWNS

10 canned anchovies
2-3 tablespoons milk
75 g (3 oz) butter
1 large onion,
  chopped
1-2 cloves garlic,
  very thinly sliced
150 ml (¼ pint) dry
  white wine
250 ml (8 fl oz)
  vegetable or fish
  stock (see below)
250 g (8 oz) peeled
  prawns
2 tablespoons double
  cream
salt and pepper
2-3 tablespoons
  chopped parsley
375 g (12 oz) dried
  tagliatelle
TO GARNISH:
anchovy fillets
whole prawns
Parmesan cheese,
  grated

Soak the anchovies in the milk for 30 minutes, drain, chop and set aside.

Melt 50 g (2 oz) of the butter in a pan, add the onion and cook until golden brown. Add the garlic and cook for 1 minute. Add the wine, bring to the boil and cook rapidly until reduced by half. Add the stock, anchovies, prawns, cream and salt and pepper to taste and simmer, uncovered, for 2 minutes. Remove from the heat and stir in the parsley.

Cook the pasta until al dente. Drain thoroughly and turn into a warmed serving dish. Add the remaining butter and toss well.

Heat the sauce for 1 minute, pour over the noodles and toss well. Garnish with a lattice of anchovy fillets and whole prawns. Serve immediately with Parmesan cheese.
Serves 6
NOTE: To make fish stock, place fish heads and bones in a large pan with 1 onion, 1 carrot and a bouquet garni. Cover with cold water, bring to the boil, then simmer for 1 hour; strain.

CROSTINI

Crostini, bread and cheese kebabs, are frequently served as antipasti in Italy alongside other savoury hors d'oeuvres. They are very simple to make: Spread 75 g (3 oz) garlic and parsley butter on both sides of 8 large slices of crusty, white bread, crusts removed. Layer half the bread slices with 125 g (4 oz) sliced Mozzarella cheese and top with the remaining bread. Press down firmly then cut into thick fingers, then bite-sized squares. Thread equally onto 4 small skewers. Bake in a preheated hot oven, 240°C (475°F), Gas Mark 9 for 5-10 minutes until golden. Serve at once. To ring the changes add 125 g (4 oz) salt beef with the cheese.

ITALIAN CANNELLONI

8 tubes cannelloni
FILLING:
2 tablespoons oil
1 onion, chopped
2 cloves garlic,
    crushed
250 g (8 oz) minced
    beef
4 tomatoes, skinned,
and chopped
1 tablespoon tomato
    purée
2 tablespoons red wine
salt and pepper
2 tablespoons fresh
    white breadcrumbs
25 g (1 oz) Parmesan
    cheese, grated
1 teaspoon chopped
    marjoram
1 egg, beaten
CHEESE SAUCE:
40 g (1½ oz) butter
40 g (1½ oz) flour
300 ml (½ pint)
    milk
142 ml (¼ pint)
    carton double cream
grated nutmeg
125 g (4 oz) Cheddar
    cheese, grated

To make the filling, heat the oil in a pan, add the onion and garlic and cook until golden. Add the beef and cook, stirring, until browned. Stir in the tomatoes, tomato purée, wine, and salt and pepper to taste. Cover and simmer for 30 minutes. Cool, then stir in the breadcrumbs, Parmesan, marjoram and egg.

Divide the filling between the cannelloni tubes. Place side by side in an ovenproof dish.

For the cheese sauce, melt the butter in a pan, stir in the flour and cook for 1 minute. Gradually stir in the milk. Add the cream and salt, pepper and nutmeg to taste. Add the cheese and stir until melted.

Spoon the sauce over the cannelloni. Cover and cook in a preheated moderately hot oven, 200°C (400°F), Gas Mark 6, for 25 minutes. Remove the lid and cook for a further 5 minutes or until golden brown. Serve hot.
Serves 6 to 8

ITALIAN FRIED SANDWICHES

2 teaspoons made
    mustard
8 slices buttered white
    bread, crusts
    removed
125 g (4 oz) Gruyère
    cheese, sliced
2 eggs
1 tablespoon oil
salt and pepper
oil for shallow-frying

Spread the mustard evenly over the buttered side of the bread. Arrange the cheese on 4 slices and top with the remaining bread.

Beat the eggs and oil together, adding salt and pepper to taste. Dip each sandwich into this mixture.

Heat the oil in a frying pan and fry 2 sandwiches at a time until golden brown; drain on kitchen paper. Serve immediately.
Serves 4

MIXED HORS D'OEUVRE

4 hard-boiled eggs
125 g (4 oz) smoked
    cod, cooked and
    flaked
125 g (4 oz) each
    salami, liver
    sausage and garlic
    sausage, sliced
4 large tomatoes
6 tablespoons rice
    and fruit salad
125 g (4 oz) each
    green beans and
    cauliflower, cooked
TO GARNISH:
Béchamel sauce,
    capers, sweet
    pickle, fresh herbs,
    lettuce, olives,
    onion rings

Shell and halve the eggs, scoop out the yolks and mix with the fish. Moisten with Béchamel sauce and spoon into the egg whites. Garnish with capers and arrange 2 egg halves in the centre of each of 4 plates.

Skin the cold meats and divide the slices between the plates. Slice the tomatoes, arrange them and garnish them with sweet pickle, herbs such as chives and basil and, if you like, a little French dressing. Position the lettuce leaves and spoon on the rice salad. Arrange the beans and cauliflower florets and garnish with a little Béchamel sauce. Arrange the olives and onion rings beside them.
Serves 4

SPAGHETTI WITH GARLIC OIL

500 g (1 lb) fresh
  spaghetti
8 tablespoons olive
  oil
3 cloves garlic,
  crushed
50 g (2 oz) butter
2 tablespoons
  chopped basil

Cook the spaghetti until *al dente*.

Meanwhile, heat the oil in a pan, add the garlic and fry until golden, stirring constantly.

Drain the spaghetti and turn into a warmed serving dish. Add the butter and toss well. Pour over the oil and garlic and mix well. Stir in the basil and serve immediately.

Serves 6

TAGLIATELLE WITH EGGS AND BACON

250 g (8 oz) fresh
  tagliatelle
2 tablespoons olive
  oil
125 g (4 oz) streaky
  bacon, chopped
3 eggs, beaten
1 tablespoon chopped
  parsley
3 tablespoons double
  cream
2 teaspoons snipped
  chives
1/2 teaspoon chopped
  fresh basil
salt and pepper
fresh basil leaves, to
  garnish

Cook the pasta in boiling salted water, according to the packet instructions until just tender.

Meanwhile, heat the oil in a pan, add the bacon and cook until crisp and golden.

Drain the pasta, return to the pan and immediately add the eggs, bacon with its juices and parsley. Stir briskly so that the heat of the pasta just cooks the eggs to coat the strips. When the eggs are cooked, add the cream, chives, basil and salt and pepper to taste and toss gently to mix. Serve at once, garnished with fresh basil leaves.

Serves 4

GREEN GNOCCHI

500 g (1 lb) spinach
  leaves, drained,
  squeezed dry and
  finely chopped
125 g (4 oz) butter
175 g (6 oz) ricotta
200 g (7 oz) stale
  bread, soaked in
  about 500 ml (18
  fl oz) milk and
  strained
2 eggs
salt and pepper
50 g (2 oz) Parmesan
  cheese, grated
lime or lemon slices,
  to garnish
  (optional)

Place the spinach and half of the butter in a pan and cook until the spinach is very tender and looks as if it is about to stick to the pan. Add the ricotta and cook for a further 3 minutes.

Add the strained bread mixture and eggs and mix well to a firm but not too dry mixture. Season to taste with salt and pepper. If the mixture appears a little too soft at this stage then add a little flour or dried breadcrumbs to absorb the excess moisture.

Roll into pointed sausage shapes about 2.5 cm (1 inch) in length and place on a board to dry for 1 hour.

Cook in batches, in boiling salted water, for about 4 minutes; they are cooked when they rise to the surface. Remove with a slotted spoon and place in a warmed serving dish.

Add the remaining butter and toss well to coat. Sprinkle with the Parmesan cheese. Garnish with lime or lemon slices if liked and serve immediately.

Serves 6

Tagliatelle with Eggs and Bacon; Spaghetti with Garlic Oil; Green Gnocchi

AUBERGINE PIE

500 g (1 lb)
  aubergines, sliced
salt and pepper
3 tablespoons oil
250 g (8 oz)
  Mozzarella, sliced
2 tablespoons
  breadcrumbs
TOMATO SAUCE:
1 tablespoon oil
1 clove garlic, crushed
1 large onion,
  chopped
500 g (1 lb)
  tomatoes, skinned,
  seeded and chopped
1 bouquet garni
3 tablespoons dry
  white wine
1 teaspoon
  Worcestershire
  sauce
1 tablespoon tomato
  purée

Sprinkle the aubergines with salt, place in a colander and leave for 1 hour. Rinse in cold water and dry on kitchen paper.

Meanwhile, make the sauce. Heat the oil in a pan, add the garlic and onion, fry gently until soft. Add the tomatoes and cook for 2 minutes. Add the remaining ingredients, with salt and pepper to taste. Simmer, uncovered, for 45 minutes, until thickened. Remove the bouquet garni.

Heat the oil in a frying pan, add the aubergine slices and fry until golden. Drain on kitchen paper.

Fill a shallow ovenproof dish with alternate layers of aubergines, Mozzarella and tomato sauce, finishing with cheese. Sprinkle with the breadcrumbs.

Bake in a preheated moderately hot oven, 200°C (400°F), Gas Mark 6, for 30 minutes. Serve hot or cold.
Serves 6 to 8

ITALIAN OMELETTE

2 or 3 eggs
salt and pepper
15 g (½ oz) butter
FILLING:
15 g (½ oz) butter
1 tablespoon chopped
  onion
4 black olives, pitted
1 × 230 g (8 oz) can
  chopped tomatoes
¼ teaspoon dried
  oregano

Break the eggs into a bowl, add salt and pepper to taste and beat lightly with a fork until well mixed but not frothy. Set aside.

To make the filling, melt the butter in a pan, add the onion and fry until soft. Chop the olives and add to the pan with the tomatoes and their juice, oregano and salt and pepper to taste. Simmer for 10 to 15 minutes until most of the liquid has evaporated and a thick purée forms.

To make the omelette, melt the butter in a preheated pan until sizzling. Add the eggs immediately. As the edge begins to set, draw the mixture towards the centre with a fork and, at the same time, tilt the pan slightly allowing the uncooked egg to run from the centre onto the hot base of the pan to set quickly.

When the omelette is lightly browned underneath but still soft and creamy on top, cover with the prepared filling. Fold over to enclose and turn onto a warmed serving plate. Serve immediately.
Serves 1

LEFT: *Aubergine Pie*

RIGHT: *Bacon and Mushroom Risotto;*
Pilaff with Chicken Livers and Mushrooms

PILAFF WITH CHICKEN LIVERS AND MUSHROOMS

25 g (1 oz) butter
75 g (3 oz) streaky bacon, chopped
2 cloves garlic, crushed
250 g (8 oz) chicken livers, chopped
125 g (4 oz) mushrooms, sliced
250 ml (8 fl oz) cider
1 teaspoon chopped fresh thyme
1 bay leaf
175 g (6 oz) long-grain rice
salt and pepper
300 ml (½ pint) vegetable stock
2 tablespoons cream
lemon twists and parsley, to garnish

Melt the butter in a large heavy-based pan. Add the bacon and cook until crisp and golden. Remove with a slotted spoon and reserve. Add the garlic and chicken livers to the pan juices and stir for 5 minutes.

Add the mushrooms, cider, thyme, bay leaf, rice, reserved bacon and salt and pepper, mixing well. Stir in the stock, bring to the boil, reduce the heat, cover and simmer for 12 minutes.

Remove the lid, increase the heat, and stir until the rice is just tender and all of the liquid has been absorbed. Remove and discard the bay leaf.

Just before serving, stir in the cream. Serve at once, garnished with lemon twists and sprinkled with chopped parsley.
Serves 4 to 6

BACON AND MUSHROOM RISOTTO

1 tablespoon olive oil
15 g (½ oz) butter
75 g (3 oz) bacon, diced
2 cloves garlic crushed
1 onion, sliced
175 g (6 oz) rice
300 ml (½ pint) hot vegetable stock
300 ml (½ pint) dry white wine
½ teaspoon ground turmeric
175 g (6 oz) mushrooms, sliced
25 g (1 oz) Parmesan cheese, grated
lime slices and rosemary, to garnish
salt and pepper

Heat the oil and butter in a large heavy-based pan. Add the bacon and fry until golden. Remove and reserve. Add the garlic and onion to the pan juices and cook until golden.

Add the rice and stir gently for 1 minute. Add the stock, wine, turmeric and bacon and bring to the boil. Reduce the heat and cook, uncovered, for 12-15 minutes, until just a little liquid remains.

Add the mushrooms, Parmesan cheese and salt and pepper to taste. Cook for about 3 minutes until the mushrooms are cooked and the rice is tender. Garnish with lime slices and rosemary sprigs and serve at once.
Serves 4

AUBERGINE CHEESECAKE

375 g (12 oz)
    aubergines, diced
salt and pepper
50 g (2 oz) butter
125 g (4 oz) cheese-
    flavoured biscuits,
    crushed
1 tablespoon grated
    Parmesan cheese
4 tablespoons oil
1 onion, thinly sliced
1 × 227 g (8 oz)
    packet cream
    cheese, softened
142 ml (¼ pint)
    carton soured
    cream
½ teaspoon dried
    mixed herbs
3 eggs, beaten
175 g (6 oz)
    Cheddar cheese,
    grated

Put the aubergines in a large colander, sprinkle generously with salt and leave to drain for 1 hour.

Melt the butter in a pan over a low heat. Remove from the heat and stir in the crushed biscuits and Parmesan cheese. Press into the base of a greased 20 cm (8 inch) loose-bottomed cake tin.

Heat the oil in a pan, add the onion and fry until lightly browned. Remove with a slotted spoon and set aside.

Rinse the aubergines under cold water, drain and dry on kitchen paper. Add to the pan and fry until lightly coloured. Drain thoroughly.

Blend the cream cheese and soured cream together, adding salt and pepper to taste. Stir in the herbs, eggs and Cheddar cheese. Add the onions and aubergines and mix well.

Spread over the biscuit base and bake in a preheated moderately hot oven, 190°C (375°F), Gas Mark 5, for 35 to 40 minutes, until set and golden brown. Serve hot or cold.

Serves 6 to 8

FRESH HALIBUT KEBABS

1 kg (2 lb) halibut
    steaks
8 cherry tomatoes
2 lemons, cut into
    wedges
6 tablespoons olive
    oil
1 teaspoon chopped
    oregano
1 teaspoon chopped
    marjoram
grated rind and juice
    of 1 lemon
salt and pepper

Cut the fish steaks into bite-sized cubes. Thread onto 4 large skewers alternating with the cherry tomatoes and lemon wedges.

Mix the oil with the herbs, lemon rind and juice and salt and pepper to taste. Brush the kebabs liberally with this mixture.

Cook under a preheated hot grill for about 10 minutes, basting frequently with the marinade and turning occasionally, until cooked.

Serve hot with a little rice or risotto if liked.

Serves 4

PARMA HAM WITH MELON

4 slices melon
    (Honeydew,
    Cantaloupe,
    Ogen), seeded and
    skinned
4 slices Parma ham

Wrap each slice of melon in a slice of Parma ham. Arrange the melon parcels on individual plates, and serve.

Serves 4

Aubergine Cheesecake
RIGHT: *Aubergines Baked with Garlic; Italian Marinated Courgettes*

AUBERGINES BAKED WITH GARLIC

2 large aubergines
4 cloves garlic, peeled
150 ml (¼ pint)
    olive oil
juice of ½ lemon
2 tablespoons
    chopped parsley
salt and pepper
TO GARNISH:
lime or lemon slices
parsley sprigs

Remove the stalks from the aubergines and cut the garlic cloves in thinnish slivers lengthways. Pierce the aubergines with a knife then insert the garlic slivers into the cuts.

Place directly onto the oven shelf and bake in a preheated moderately hot oven, 200°C (400°F), Gas Mark 6, for 25-30 minutes or until the skins wrinkle and the flesh shrinks and feels soft to the touch. Remove from the oven and leave to stand for 5 minutes.

Cut the aubergines into bite-sized pieces and place in a serving dish. Beat the oil with the lemon juice, parsley and salt and pepper to taste and pour over the aubergines to coat. Serve hot or cold, garnished with lime or lemon slices and parsley.
Serves 4 to 6

ITALIAN MARINATED COURGETTES

2 tablespoons olive
    oil
2 cloves garlic,
    crushed
2 shallots, finely
    chopped
300 ml (½ pint) dry
    white wine
1 bay leaf
1 sprig fresh basil
juice of ½ lemon
375 g (12 oz)
    courgettes, sliced
salt and pepper
3 tomatoes, skinned,
    seeded and chopped
1 teaspoon chopped
    rosemary
2 teaspoons chopped
    parsley

Heat the oil in a pan, add the garlic and shallots and cook until softened. Add the wine, bring to the boil and cook until reduced by about half.

Add the bay leaf, basil, lemon juice, courgettes and salt and pepper to taste, mixing well. Cook until the courgettes are just tender, about 5 minutes. Remove from the heat and stir in the tomatoes. Leave until cold.

Remove and discard the bay leaf and basil sprig. Cover and chill for at least 2 hours. Serve sprinkled with the chopped rosemary and parsley.
Serves 4 to 6

MINI PIZZAS

½ × 567 g (20 oz)
    packet white or
    brown bread mix
2 tablespoons oil
2 onions, finely
    chopped
2 cloves garlic,
    crushed
1 × 800 g (1 lb
    10 oz) can peeled
    tomatoes
1 × 140 g (5 oz) can
    tomato purée
2 teaspoons dried
    mixed herbs
salt and pepper
TO GARNISH:
1 × 50 g (2 oz) can
    anchovy fillets,
    drained
50 g (2 oz) small
    black olives, pitted
    and sliced
chopped parsley

Make up the bread mix following the packet instructions and leave to rise.

Heat the oil in a frying pan, add the onions and garlic and fry gently until soft. Chop the tomatoes and add to the pan, with their juice, the tomato purée, herbs, and salt and pepper to taste. Simmer until the mixture begins to thicken.

Roll out the bread dough to a 5 mm (¼ inch) thickness and cut into 6 cm (2½ inch) rounds with a plain cutter. Place well apart on greased baking sheets and divide the tomato mixture between the pizzas. Bake in a preheated hot oven, 220°C (425°F), Gas Mark 7, for 10 to 15 minutes, until risen and golden.

Top each pizza with a circle of anchovy fillet, an olive slice and parsley. Serve hot or cold.
Makes about 50

VEAL AND SPINACH LOAF

500 g (1 lb) spinach
500 g (1 lb) braising
    veal
125 g (4 oz) ham
1 onion
75 g (3 oz) Parmesan
    cheese, grated
2 eggs, beaten
25 g (1 oz) fresh
    breadcrumbs
parsley sprigs to
    garnish

Cook the spinach gently, with just the water clinging to the leaves after washing, for 5 minutes; drain well.

Place the veal, ham and onion in a processor or blender. Chop finely, then transfer to a mixing bowl.

Process the spinach for 5 seconds and add to the mixing bowl.

Add the cheese with the eggs and breadcrumbs; mix well.

Transfer to a greased 1 kg (2 lb) loaf tin or terrine and cook in a preheated moderate oven, 160°C (325°F), Gas Mark 3, for 1 hour.

Turn out and serve sliced, hot or cold. Garnish with parsley sprigs.
Serves 6

Veal and Spinach Loaf

BACON PIZZA FINGERS

1 × 567 g (20 oz)
    packet white bread
    mix
75 g (3 oz) butter
500 g (1 lb) onions,
    chopped
4 cloves garlic,
    crushed
2 × 397 g (14 oz)
    can of chopped
    tomatoes
2 teaspoons dried
    mixed herbs
salt and pepper
500 g (1 lb) streaky
    bacon, derinded

Make up the bread mix according to the packet instructions. Divide in half. Roll out each piece to fit a 35 × 25 cm (14 × 10 inch) greased baking sheet.

Melt the butter in a pan, add the onions and garlic and fry until translucent. Spread over the dough.

Mix the tomatoes and juice with the herbs and salt and pepper to taste, then spread over the onions. Top with bacon.

Bake in a preheated hot oven, 230°C (450°F), Gas Mark 8, for 10 minutes. Lower the heat to 180°C (350°F), Gas Mark 4, and bake for a further 30 minutes.

Serve warm, cut into fingers.
Serves 20

RIGHT: *Marinated Artichoke Hearts; Sicilian Sweet-Sour Vegetables*

MARINATED ARTICHOKES

2 × 400 g (13 oz)
    can artichoke
    hearts
4 tablespoons lemon
    juice
125 ml (4 fl oz) dry
    white wine
450 ml (¾ pint)
    water
2 tablespoons white
    wine vinegar
2 bay leaves
1 clove garlic, bruised
DRESSING:
5 tablespoons olive
    oil
2 tablespoons lemon
    juice
1 clove garlic, crushed
salt and pepper
2 tablespoons
    chopped parsley

Dip the artichokes in the lemon juice then place in a pan with the wine, water, vinegar, 1 bay leaf and the bruised garlic. Bring to the boil, reduce the heat and simmer until tender, about 10 minutes. Drain and place in a serving dish with the remaining bay leaf.

To make the dressing, beat the oil with the lemon juice, garlic and salt and pepper to taste. Spoon over the dressing and leave to marinate for 30 minutes. Toss to mix before serving, sprinkled with chopped parsley.
Serves 4

SICILIAN VEGETABLES

3 large aubergines
salt and pepper
4 celery sticks
6 tablespoons olive oil
1 large onion, chopped
1 × 397 g (14 oz)
    can chopped
    tomatoes, drained
    and sieved
1 tablespoon tomato
    purée
2-3 tablespoons white
    wine vinegar
2 tablespoons sugar
2 tablespoons capers
12 green olives, pitted
TO GARNISH:
1 tablespoon pine
    kernels or flaked
    almonds
2 hard-boiled eggs,
    quartered

Cut the aubergines into 1 cm (½ inch) cubes. Sprinkle with salt, put into a colander, cover and leave for 1 hour. Rinse and dry with kitchen paper.

Cook the celery in boiling water for 6 to 8 minutes. Drain and cut into 1 cm (½ inch) cubes.

Heat 4 tablespoons of the oil in a large frying pan, add the aubergine and fry quickly, stirring frequently, for about 10 minutes until tender.

Heat the remaining oil in a large pan, add the onion and fry gently for 5 minutes. Add the celery and fry, stirring, for 5 minutes. Add the tomatoes, tomato purée and a little salt and pepper. Simmer gently for about 5 minutes. Add 2 tablespoons of vinegar, the sugar, capers, olives and aubergine. Simmer for a few minutes, stirring. Cool, cover and chill until needed. Serve garnished with pine kernels and egg.
Serves 4

FISH

The local coast fish markets of Italy are literally teeming with an amazing variety of fish and shellfish throughout the year. The Italian housewife can choose to cook fresh anchovies, sardines, sea bass, sea bream, cod, halibut, mackerel, red and grey mullet, monkfish, sole, tuna, squid, cuttlefish, whiting, eel, carp, trout, tench, scampi, whitebait, mussels, hake and octopus – to name but a few – on almost any day of the year.

The freshness of the fish has created little need for complicated cooking methods, elaborate sauces or fancy garnishes. The recipes chosen here therefore reflect basic poaching, grilling, barbecuing, baking and casseroling methods and the sauces are simple affairs designed to complement rather than overpower the delicate taste and texture of the finished fish dish.

Fresh fish that has been fried in batter or breadcrumbs and fish incorporated into sauces for serving over pasta are nearly always served with a simple green salad; fish casseroles, soups and stews with a hearty if somewhat rustic flat crusty bread; poached fish with a seasonal vegetable selection and plain cooked potatoes; and grilled or barbecued fish with wedges of lemon for squeezing.

TUNA CIABATTA SLICES

1 ciabatta loaf
4-6 tablespoons
    tomato pizza sauce
1 orange, peeled and
    thinly sliced
125 g (4 oz) canned
    tuna in olive oil
125 g (4 oz)
    Mozzarella
    cheese, thinly
    sliced
salt and pepper
50 g (2 oz) black
    olives, halved
few sprigs fresh
    oregano or
    marjoram

Cut the ciabatta loaf through the middle horizontally, so that you have two flat halves. Spread evenly with the tomato sauce and arrange the orange slices on top. Drain the tuna, reserving the oil, and scatter flakes or small chunks of fish over the oranges. Top with the cheese slices and drizzle with the reserved tuna oil. Sprinkle with salt and pepper to taste then top with the olives and small sprigs of oregano.

Bake in a preheated moderate oven, 180°C (350°F), Gas Mark 4, for 15-20 minutes until the cheese has melted and the bread is crispy. Serve hot cut into thick slices.
Serves 4

HADDOCK AND SPINACH LAYER

500 g (1 lb) haddock
    fillets
150 ml (¼ pint)
    skimmed milk
1 bay leaf
salt and pepper
1 hard-boiled egg,
    chopped
500 g (1 lb) frozen
    leaf spinach
SAUCE:
150 ml (¼ pint)
    skimmed milk
    (approximately)
25 g (1 oz)
    margarine
1 onion, chopped
25 g (1 oz) plain
    flour
grated nutmeg
TOPPING:
2 crispbreads, crushed
1 tomato, sliced, to
    garnish

Place the haddock in a pan. Add the milk, bay leaf, salt and pepper to taste, then poach for about 10 minutes until the fish is tender. Drain, reserving the liquor. Flake the haddock and mix with the egg.

Cook the spinach as directed on the packet and drain well.

Make the fish liquor up to 300 ml (½ pint) with extra milk. Melt the margarine in a pan and fry the onion until soft. Stir in the flour and cook for 1 minute. Gradually blend in the milk then bring to the boil, stirring continuously. Cook, stirring, for a further 1 minute. Season to taste with salt, pepper and nutmeg. Stir in the fish and egg mixture; mix well.

Layer the spinach and fish mixture in a greased 1.2 litre (2 pint) ovenproof dish, finishing with a layer of spinach. Sprinkle with the crispbreads and cook in a preheated moderate oven, 180°C (350°F), Gas Mark 4, for 20-30 minutes.

Garnish with tomato slices.
Serves 4

GRILLED SEAFOOD

16 fresh mussels
250 g (8 oz)
    monkfish, boned
    and cubed
16 extra large prawns
50 ml (2 fl oz) dry
    white wine
4 tablespoons fresh
    white breadcrumbs
2 cloves garlic, finely
    chopped
3 tablespoons
    chopped parsley
salt and pepper
8 tablespoons olive
    oil
juice of ½ lemon

Clean and scrub the shellfish thoroughly. Heat half of the oil in a large frying pan, add the mussels, monkfish and prawns and fry over a high heat until the mussels have opened, adding the wine after about 2 minutes and stirring and tossing frequently.

Arrange the mussels, prawns and monkfish in a single layer in a large flameproof gratin dish. Mix the breadcrumbs with the garlic, parsley and salt and pepper to taste. Sprinkle over the seafood then drizzle over the oil and lemon juice.

Cook under a preheated hot grill for about 2-3 minutes until the topping is crisp and golden and the fish is thoroughly cooked.
Serves 4

Haddock and Spinach Layer

ITALIAN COD STEAKS

2 tablespoons olive
oil
2 cloves garlic,
crushed
1 teaspoon ground
coriander
juice of 2 oranges
juice of ½ lemon
4 cod steaks
1 onion, thinly sliced
1 canned pimiento, or
cooked red pepper,
drained and thinly
sliced
TO GARNISH:
2 oranges, peeled,
pith removed and
segmented
chopped parsley

Mix 1 tablespoon of the olive oil with the garlic, coriander, orange and lemon juice. Lay the cod steaks in a lightly-greased ovenproof dish, large enough to take them in one layer, and pour over the orange juice mixture. Cover and chill for 1-2 hours.

Meanwhile, fry the onion gently in the remaining oil until soft but not coloured. Spoon over the fish with the pimiento.

Bake in a preheated moderately hot oven, 200°C (400°F), Gas Mark 6, for 15-20 minutes, or until the fish is opaque and flakes when touched with the point of a knife.

Garnish with the orange segments and chopped parsley. Serve with boiled rice or pasta.
Serves 4

MEDITERRANEAN FISH STEAKS

4 tablespoons olive
oil
2 onions, thinly sliced
1 clove garlic, finely
chopped
1 green pepper,
cored, seeded and
sliced in rings
4 large tomatoes,
skinned and sliced
2 teaspoons dried
basil
salt and pepper
4 white fish steaks
2 teaspoons lemon
juice
6 tablespoons dry
white wine

Heat the oil in a frying pan and fry the onions and garlic until softened. Add the green pepper rings and continue frying for 3 minutes. Remove from the heat and place half the mixture in a casserole.

Arrange half the tomato slices on top and sprinkle with half the basil and salt and pepper to taste. Place the fish steaks on top and sprinkle with the lemon juice. Add the rest of the tomato slices, basil and onion and green pepper mixture. Pour in the wine.

Cover and cook in a preheated moderate oven, 180°C (350°F), Gas Mark 4, for about 45 minutes or until the fish is tender.
Serves 4

MACARONI FISH SALAD

500 g (1 lb) dried
short-cut macaroni
salt and pepper
300 ml (½ pint)
mayonnaise
300 ml (½ pint)
milk
250 ml (8 fl oz)
vinaigrette dressing
1 kg (2 lb) white fish
fillets, cooked,
skinned and flaked
250 g (8 oz) peeled
prawns
6 celery sticks, thinly
sliced
8 spring onions,
chopped
500 g (1 lb) white
cabbage, cored and
shredded
TO GARNISH:
1 hard-boiled egg,
sliced
watercress

Cook the macaroni in boiling salted water according to the packet instructions. Drain and cool. Mix together the mayonnaise, milk, vinaigrette dressing and salt and pepper to taste, then fold in the macaroni. Add the fish, prawns, celery, spring onions and cabbage and fold together thoroughly. Pile into a serving dish and chill.

Serve garnished with egg slices and watercress.
Serves 16

Macaroni Fish Salad

SEAFOOD TAGLIATELLE

284 ml (½ pint)
    carton single cream
2 strips of lemon peel
75 g (3 oz) butter
1 onion, finely
    chopped
50 g (2 oz) plain
    flour
600 ml (1 pint) milk
1 bay leaf
pinch of grated
    nutmeg
750 g (1½ lb)
    skinless cod fillet,
    cubed
250 g (8 oz) peeled
    prawns
1 fennel bulb,
    chopped
2 teaspoons chopped
    fresh fennel leaves
salt and pepper
125 g (8 oz) Gruyere
    cheese, grated
750 g (1½ lb) fresh
    tagliatelle
whole shell-on
    prawns, to garnish

Place the cream in a pan with the lemon peel. Heat gently until hot but not boiling then remove from the heat and leave to stand for 10 minutes. Remove and discard the lemon peel.

Melt the butter in a pan, add the onion and cook until softened. Stir in the flour and cook for 1 minute. Gradually add the cream and milk mixing well. Bring to the boil, stirring constantly, until the mixture is smooth and thickened. Add the bay leaf and nutmeg and simmer gently for 5 minutes. Remove and discard the bay leaf.

Meanwhile, cook the fennel in boiling water for 2 minutes then drain thoroughly. Add to the sauce with the cod, prawns, fennel leaves and salt and pepper to taste. Continue to cook the sauce over a gentle heat until the fish is cooked, about 5-8 minutes. Stir in the cheese and stir to melt and blend.

Meanwhile, cook the tagliatelle in boiling salted water, according to the packet instructions, until just tender. Drain and place on a heated serving plate. Spoon over the prepared sauce and garnish with whole prawns to serve.

Serves 6

ITALIAN SEAFOOD LOAF

BASE:
1 large Harvest grain
    loaf
2 cloves garlic
6 tablespoons olive
    oil
4 tablespoons wine
    vinegar
SALAD:
250 g (8 oz) cooked
    peeled prawns
3 carrots, sliced
1 small cauliflower,
    divided into florets
50 g (2 oz) green
    beans, trimmed
400 g (14 oz) can
    artichoke hearts,
    drained and
    chopped
3 celery sticks,
    chopped
6 black olives, pitted
6 green olives, pitted
SAUCE:
50 g (2 oz) fresh
    breadcrumbs
50 g (2 oz) chopped
    parsley
2 teaspoons capers
2 cloves garlic
50 g (2 oz) can
    anchovy fillets
juice of 1 lemon
about 6 tablespoons
    olive oil
pepper

To make the base, cut the crusts off the loaf and cut into three large slices lengthwise. Place in a moderate oven, 180°C (350°F), Gas Mark 4 for about 2 hours or until very crisp. Rub with the garlic cloves and lay flat on a serving dish. Pour over the oil and vinegar and leave to stand for 2 hours.

To make the salad, cook the carrots, cauliflower and green beans in a pan of boiling salted water for 5 minutes. Drain well then mix with the artichokes, celery and olives.

To make the sauce, soak the breadcrumbs in cold water for 5 minutes then drain and squeeze dry. Place the parsley, capers, garlic, anchovy fillets and their oil in a blender. With the blender on a medium speed, gradually add the oil, bread, lemon juice and pepper to taste and process to a smooth sauce, adding a little more oil if the consistency is too thick.

To assemble, put layers of the prawns, sauce and vegetables on top of each prepared base, finishing with a layer of the sauce. Chill for at least 30 minutes before serving. Cut into slices and serve.

Serves 6

THE TASTE OF TOMATOES

Tomatoes are one of the most characteristic of all Italian ingredients, and are widely used in the country's cuisine. There are various ways to accentuate that delicious tomato taste. One obvious method, of course, is to add a few teaspoons of concentrated tomato purée to tomato sauces. If you don't have any of this at hand, though, try a teaspoon of sugar, a dash of Worcestershire sauce, or a little grated orange rind.

RIGHT: *Venetian-Style Red Mullet; Italian Fish Mayonnaise*

VENETIAN-STYLE RED MULLET

5 tablespoons olive oil

1 large onion, chopped

300 ml (½ pint) dry white wine

1½ tablespoons wine vinegar

1-2 mint sprigs

2 cloves garlic, chopped

4 red mullet, cleaned

flour for coating

salt and pepper

TO GARNISH:

orange and lemon slices

mint sprigs

Heat 2 tablespoons of the oil in a pan, add the onion and fry gently until soft but not coloured. Add the wine and vinegar and boil briskly for 10 minutes or until reduced by half.

Meanwhile, put 2 or 3 mint leaves and a little garlic inside each fish. Season the flour well with salt and pepper and use to coat the fish.

Heat the remaining oil in a shallow frying pan, add the fish and fry gently until crisp, golden and cooked through, about 6 minutes on each side. Drain and arrange in a shallow dish. Pour over the hot sauce and leave to cool, basting occasionally.

Serve cold, garnished with orange and lemon slices and mint.

Serves 4

ITALIAN FISH MAYONNAISE

625 g (1¼ lb) white fish fillets (e.g. cod, haddock, rockfish)

salt and pepper

2 lemon slices

3-4 tablespoons olive oil

2 teaspoons lemon juice

250 g (8 oz) frozen mixed vegetables

50 g (2 oz) peeled prawns

200 ml (7 fl oz) Mayonnaise (see page 152)

TO GARNISH:

2 hard-boiled eggs, sliced

stuffed olives, sliced

Put the fish in a pan and cover with cold water. Add 1 teaspoon salt and 2 lemon slices. Bring to simmering point and poach for 5 minutes or until cooked. Drain, skin and chop the fish. While still hot, flavour to taste with oil, salt, pepper and lemon juice. Cover and leave to cool.

Cook the vegetables as directed on the packet, drain and cool. Transfer to a serving dish and top with the fish and half the prawns. Pour over the Mayonnaise, thinning with water if necessary. Garnish with the remaining prawns, the eggs and olives.

Serves 4

SALT COD AND CELERY BAKE

500 g (1 lb) dried salt
  cod, soaked
  overnight, or 625 g
  (1¼ lb) cod fillet
40 g (1½ oz) butter
40 g (1½ oz) plain
  flour
450 ml (¾ pint)
  milk (or half fish
  stock and half
  milk)
pinch of dry mustard
salt and pepper
1 egg, beaten
125 g (4 oz) fresh
  breadcrumbs
4 celery sticks, finely
  chopped
tomato slices to
  garnish

Drain the salt cod, if using. Place the fish in a saucepan. Cover with fresh water and bring to the boil. Simmer for 20 minutes, then drain well. Skin, bone and flake the fish.

Melt the butter in another saucepan. Add the flour and cook, stirring, for 2 minutes. Gradually stir in the milk (or stock and milk) and bring to the boil. Simmer, stirring, until thickened. Add the mustard and salt and pepper to taste. Remove from the heat and cool slightly, then beat in the egg.

Place half the cod in a greased baking dish. Cover with half the breadcrumbs, half the celery, then half the sauce. Repeat the layers.

Cook in a preheated moderately hot oven, 190°C (375°F), Gas Mark 5, for 20 minutes. Garnish with tomato slices.
Serves 4

TAGLIATELLE WITH PRAWN SAUCE

500 g (1 lb) shell-on
  prawns
1 onion, sliced
2 stalks parsley
1 stick celery, sliced
6 to 8 black pepper-
  corns
150 ml (¼ pint)
  water
150 ml (¼ pint) dry
  white wine
50 g (2 oz) butter
4 shallots or small
  onions, chopped
2 teaspoons plain
  flour
200 ml (7 fl oz)
  carton
  crème fraîche
pinch chilli powder
salt and pepper
500 g (1 lb) fresh
  tagliatelle
TO GARNISH:
1 tablespoon chopped
  parsley
shell-on prawns

Shell the prawns, reserving 4 or 5 whole. Cover the prawns and set aside in the refrigerator.

Place the prawn shells in a pan with the onion, parsley stalks, celery and peppercorns and pour on the water and wine. Bring to the boil and simmer for 20 minutes. Strain through a sieve and discard the contents. Return the liquid to the cleaned pan. Boil until it is reduced to 3 tablespoons, then pour off and reserve the liquid.

Melt 25 g (1 oz) of the butter in the pan, add the shallots or onions and cook for 4 minutes. Stir in the flour and cook for 1 minute. Pour on the reserved liquid, stirring, and the crème fraîche. Stir until smooth, then add the shelled prawns and heat gently. Season to taste with chilli powder, salt and pepper.

Cook the tagliatelle until al dente. Drain and turn on to a warmed serving dish. Toss with the remaining butter, pour the sauce over, sprinkle on the parsley and garnish with the whole prawns.
Serves 4

Tagliatelle with Prawn Sauce

ITALIAN BAKED SEA BASS

1 × 1.5 kg (3½ lb)
  sea bass, cleaned
  and scaled
2 large onions, sliced
4 tablespoons olive
  oil
2 cloves garlic,
  crushed
2 teaspoons chopped
  fresh rosemary
3 tablespoons
  chopped parsley
2 tablespoons
  chopped fresh basil
grated rind and juice
  of 1 lemon
4 tablespoons dry
  white wine
salt and pepper
450 ml (¾ pint)
  mayonnaise

Wash the sea bass thoroughly then dry with kitchen paper. Place the onions on a large sheet of foil then sprinkle with half of the oil. Coat the inside and skin of the sea bass with the garlic and herbs, reserving 1 tablespoon of the parsley. Place the fish on top of the onions and sprinkle with the lemon rind, lemon juice, remaining oil, wine and salt and pepper to taste. Fold over the foil to enclose the fish completely then place on a baking sheet or in an ovenproof dish.

Bake in a preheated moderate oven, 180°C (350°F), Gas Mark 4 for 30 minutes. Remove from the oven and allow to cool completely, without opening the foil parcel.

When cool, transfer the fish to a serving plate, reserving the juices. Strain the juices into a pan and boil to reduce to about 2-3 tablespoons. Allow to cool then whisk gradually into the mayonnaise. Add the remaining chopped parsley and serve with the fish.
Serves 6

HERB COD BAKE

4 cod steaks
2 teaspoons lemon
  juice
pepper
15 g (½ oz) butter
1 onion, finely
  chopped
1 green pepper,
  cored, deseeded and
  chopped
3 celery sticks,
  chopped
6 tomatoes, skinned
  and chopped
garlic salt
½ teaspoon dried
  basil
parsley sprigs to
  garnish

Wash and dry the steaks and place in a shallow, ovenproof dish. Sprinkle with the lemon juice and pepper to taste.

Melt the butter in a pan and lightly fry the onion, green pepper and celery. Add the tomatoes, garlic salt to taste, and basil. Bring to the boil, cover and simmer for 10 to 15 minutes.

Spoon the vegetables over the fish, cover with foil and cook in a preheated moderate oven 180°C (350°F), Gas Mark 4, for 30 minutes. Serve garnished with parsley.
Serves 4

Herb Cod Bake

TAGLIATELLE WITH SHELLFISH AND BROCCOLI

375 g (12 oz)
    broccoli
2 tablespoons oil
1 onion, chopped
1 clove garlic, crushed
125 g (4 oz) button
    mushrooms, sliced
250 g (8 oz) scallops
175 g (6 oz) peeled
    prawns
150 ml (¼ pint) dry
    vermouth
284 ml (½ pint)
    carton double
    cream
1 tablespoon chopped
    parsley
1 teaspoon chopped
    marjoram
salt and pepper
75 g (12 oz) dried
    tagliatelle verdi
grated Pecorino
    cheese, to serve

Break the broccoli into small florets and cook in boiling water for 3 minutes. Drain and leave to cool.

Heat the oil in a large heavy-based pan, add the onion and garlic and fry until softened. Stir in the mushrooms, scallops, prawns and vermouth. Bring to the boil and cook until only about 2 tablespoons of the vermouth remains. Add the cream, parsley, marjoram, broccoli and salt and pepper to taste.

Meanwhile, cook the tagliatelle in boiling salted water, according to the packet instructions until just tender. Drain and place in a heated serving dish. Pour over the shellfish and broccoli sauce and serve at once with grated Pecorino cheese.
Serves 4 to 6

ITALIAN GRILLED MACKEREL

4 mackerel, weighing
    about 375 g
    (12 oz) each,
    cleaned
150 ml (¼ pint)
    olive oil
juice of 1 lemon
2 tablespoons
    chopped fresh
    oregano
salt and pepper
3 tablespoons dried
    breadcrumbs
lemon wedges, to
    serve

Wash and dry the fish and place in a shallow flameproof dish. Mix the oil with the lemon juice and brush over the fish. Sprinkle both sides of the fish with the oregano, salt and pepper to taste and breadcrumbs. Cover and leave to stand for 2 hours.

Cook the fish under a preheated hot grill until cooked, turning over once, about 8-10 minutes. Serve hot with wedges of lemon.
Serves 4

Tagliatelle with Shellfish and Broccoli; Spaghetti with Tuna

SPAGHETTI WITH TUNA

4 tablespoons olive
  oil
2-3 cloves garlic,
  crushed
1 kg (2 lb) tomatoes,
  skinned, deseeded
  and chopped
1 tablespoon each
  chopped basil and
  oregano
salt and pepper
2 × 198 g (7 oz)
  can of tuna fish,
  drained and flaked
1 teaspoon anchovy
  essence
2 teaspoons capers
  (optional)
500 g (1 lb) fresh
  spaghetti
25 g (1 oz) butter
oregano or basil
  sprigs to garnish
  (optional)

Heat the oil in a pan, add the garlic and cook until golden brown, stirring occasionally. Add the tomatoes, herbs, and pepper to taste. Bring to the boil and simmer, uncovered, for 30 minutes, until thickened. Add the tuna, anchovy essence and capers, if using.

Cook the spaghetti until *al dente*. Drain thoroughly, turn into a warmed serving dish, add the butter and toss well.

Taste the sauce and add salt if necessary, then spoon over the pasta. Garnish with oregano or basil if liked, and serve immediately.
Serves 4 to 6

RED MULLET WITH FENNEL

1 large bulb fennel
25 g (1 oz) unsalted
  butter
1 small onion, sliced
1 shallot, finely sliced
2 teaspoons lemon
  juice
salt and pepper
4 small red mullet,
  cleaned and scaled
TO GARNISH:
dill sprigs
lemon wedges

Trim the base of the fennel. Wash and slice the remaining fennel into thin rounds.

Melt the butter in a pan, stir in the onion, shallot, fennel, lemon juice, and salt and pepper to taste. Cover and cook for 5 minutes.

Spoon into an ovenproof dish. Place the red mullet on top and sprinkle with salt and pepper. Cover with foil and cook in a preheated moderate oven, 180°C (350°F), Gas Mark 4, for 20 minutes or until cooked. Garnish with dill and lemon to serve.
Serves 4
VARIATION: Replace the fennel with blanched chicory.

GRILLED SCAMPI

24 large scampi
50 ml (2 fl oz) olive
  oil
juice of ½ lemon
3 tablespoons grated
  Parmesan cheese
25 g (1 oz) fresh
  breadcrumbs
salt

Cut the scampi almost in half lengthways and open out to reveal the flesh. Mix the oil with the lemon juice and brush over the flesh liberally. Mix the cheese with the breadcrumbs and salt to taste. Sprinkle over the scampi to coat.

Cook under a preheated hot grill until golden and cooked, about 4-5 mintues.
Serves 4

SALMON AND ORANGE PASTA

500 g (1 lb) salmon
  fillet, skinned
4 spring onions
250 g (8 oz) dried
  tagliatelle or
  fettucine
4 large oranges
1 tablespoon
  cornflour
pepper
parsley sprigs, to
  garnish

Cut the salmon into strips about 1 cm (½ inch) wide. Trim and slice the spring onions. Cook the pasta in boiling, salted water until just tender.

Meanwhile, using a sharp knife, cut all the peel and white pith away from 2 oranges and carefully remove the segments, catching the juice in a bowl. Squeeze the juice from the remaining 2 oranges, and if necessary make the juice up to 250 ml (8 fl oz) with cold water.

Blend the cornflour with 3 tablespoons of the juice and place the remainder in a wide saucepan. Bring almost to the boil, add the salmon strips and poach gently for 2-3 minutes. Lift out carefully with a slotted spoon and keep hot.

Stir the onions and blended cornflour into the pan and heat until boiling, stirring constantly. Cook for 1 minute then season with pepper to taste. Add the salmon and orange segments. Drain the pasta and place in a heated serving dish. Spoon the salmon mixture over and serve at once, garnished with parsley sprigs.
Serves 4

ITALIAN HERBY MUSSELS

25 g (1 oz) butter
2 tablespoons oil
4 celery sticks, sliced
1 red and 1 yellow
    pepper, cored,
    deseeded and diced
2 cloves garlic,
    crushed
5 cm (2 inch) strip of
    lemon rind
1 bay leaf
2 kg (4 lb) fresh
    mussels, scrubbed
    clean
6 tablespoons dry
    white wine
salt and pepper
125 g (4 oz) fresh
    white breadcrumbs
4 eggs
2 tablespoons single
    cream
¼ teaspoon turmeric
2 tablespoons grated
    Parmesan cheese
tomato quarters to
    garnish

Heat the butter and oil in a shallow, flameproof casserole. Add the celery and peppers and fry until softened.

Add the garlic, lemon rind, bay leaf, mussels (check that none are opened), and wine. Season with salt and pepper to taste.

Cover and cook over high heat for 2 to 3 minutes, shaking the pan constantly. Remove the opened mussels, cover the pan and cook for 1 minute. Discard any mussels which have not opened. Drain and reserve the liquid from the casserole.

Pull off and discard the empty top shell from each mussel. Return the mussels to the casserole, and sprinkle with the breadcrumbs.

Beat together the eggs, cream, 6 tablespoons of the reserved cooking liquor, turmeric, and salt and pepper to taste. Pour over the mussels and scatter the cheese on top. Cook in a preheated moderately hot oven, 200°C (400°F), Gas Mark 6, for 10 to 15 minutes, until set and golden.

Garnish with tomato quarters.
Serves 4

SALMON WITH CELERY AND FENNEL

250 g (8 oz) celery,
    sliced
250 g (8 oz) fennel,
    sliced
600 ml (1 pint) water
    or fish stock
½ teaspoon celery
    salt
2 slices of lemon
4 salmon tailpiece
    fillets (weighing
    about 125 g/4 oz
    each)
2 teaspoons arrowroot
    powder or
    cornflower
pepper
TO GARNISH:
grated lemon rind
tomato slices
celery leaves
chopped parsley

Place the celery and fennel in a wide saucepan or deep frying pan with stock or water. Bring to the boil, add the celery salt and lemon slices, cover, reduce the heat and simmer gently for about 8 minutes.

Carefully lower the salmon into the pan, cover and allow to simmer very gently for a further 4–5 minutes.

Remove the salmon and vegetables with a slotted spooon and keep hot. Remove and discard the lemon slices. Boil the liquid rapidly to reduce to about 300 ml (½ pint). Blend the arrowroot or cornflour with a little cold water and stir into the pan. Cook, stirring constantly, until thickened. Season with pepper to taste.

To serve, arrange the salmon with the vegetables on a heated serving plate and pour over the sauce. Garnish with grated lemon rind, tomato slices, celery leaves and chopped parsley.
Serves 4

ABOVE: *Italian Herby Mussels*

RED MULLET WITH CAPER AND OLIVE SAUCE

4 red mullet, cleaned
salt and pepper
2 tablespoons olive
    oil
1 tablespoon chopped
    fresh marjoram
4 teaspoons chopped
    parsley
40 g (1½ oz) butter
2 tablespoon capers
12 black olives,
    pitted and sliced
grated zest of ½
    lemon

Clean and dry the fish then sprinkle the insides with salt. Heat the oil in a large heavy-based frying pan, add the marjoram, half of the parsley and mullet and fry over a moderate heat for about 10 minutes, turning over once, or until cooked.

Meanwhile, melt the butter in a small pan then cook until it turns a light brown colour. Remove from the heat and stir in the capers, olives, lemon zest, remaining parsley and salt and pepper to taste.

Remove the fish from the pan with a slotted spoon and place on a heated serving dish. Spoon over the hot caper and olive sauce and serve at once.
Serves 4

BAKED SOLE WITH COURGETTES

50 g (2 oz) butter
2 tablespoons oil
8 small sole fillets
375 g (12 oz)
    courgettes, sliced
1 teaspoon chopped
    fresh rosemary
1 teaspoon chopped
    fresh basil
400 g (13 oz) can
    passata or creamed
    tomatoes
salt and pepper
4 tablespoons dried
    white breadcrumbs
juice of ½ lemon

Melt 40 g (1½ oz) of the butter and the oil in a heavy-based frying pan. Add the fish fillets and fry until golden on both sides. Remove with a slotted spoon and place in a shallow ovenproof dish.

Add the courgettes to the pan juices and cook until lightly browned. Add the rosemary, basil, passata and salt and pepper to taste. Mix well and cook for a further 3 minutes. Spoon evenly over the fish fillets.

Sprinkle with the breadcrumbs, dot with the remaining butter and drizzle with the lemon juice. Bake in a preheated hot oven 220°C (425°F), Gas Mark 7, for 10-15 minutes, or until crisp, bubbly and golden on the top. Serve at once.
Serves 4

SAVOURY SARDINES WITH HERB BUTTER

12 fresh sardines
salt and pepper
2 tablespoons flour
1 egg
2 tablespoons milk
125 g (4 oz) dried
    breadcrumbs
50 g (2 oz) butter
1 teaspoon chopped
    parsley
1 small shallot, finely
    chopped
½ clove garlic,
    crushed
2 tablespoons oil

Slit the sardines open on one side and clean thoroughly, removing the backbones but leaving the heads and tails intact.

Season the flour. Coat the sardines lightly in the seasoned flour. Beat the egg with the milk. Dip in the sardines and coat well with the breadcrumbs.

Heat the butter with the parsley, shallot, garlic and oil in a frying pan until hot. Add the sardines and cook on both sides until golden brown and cooked through, about 2-3 minutes on each side. Drain on absorbent kitchen paper and serve at once.
Serves 4

VENETIAN DRESSED CRAB

2 cooked crabs,
    weighing about
1 kg (2 lb) each
3-4 tablespoons olive
    oil
juice of 1 lemon
salt and pepper

To prepare the crabs, twist off the claws and legs then crack open to remove all the crab meat. Remove any brown and white meat from the body shells, removing and discarding the grey stomach sacs and the feathered gills. Trim and wash the shells and reserve.

Flake the crab meat into a bowl and add the oil, lemon juice and salt and pepper to taste. Mix gently to blend. Pile this mixture neatly back into the prepared crab shells and serve as soon as possible.
Serves 4

PAN FRIED TROUT WITH FENNEL

125 g (4 oz) sliced
    Parma ham
4 trout, cleaned
4 tablespoons olive
    oil
5 tablespoons soured
    cream
2 tablespoons
    chopped fresh
    fennel leaves
4 tablespoons natural
    yogurt
¼ teaspoon cornflour
40 g (1½ oz) butter
½ teaspoon lemon
    juice
salt and pepper
fennel sprigs, to
    garnish

Wrap a slice of Parma ham around each trout and secure with wooden cocktail sticks. Heat the oil in a large frying pan, add the trout and fry gently on both sides until cooked, about 5-8 minutes.

Meanwhile, to make the sauce, heat the soured cream with the fennel in a small pan but do not allow to boil. Mix the natural yogurt with the cornflour and stir into the soured cream mixture. Heat gently until the sauce thickens but only allow to simmer do not boil. Remove from the heat and whisk in small pieces of the butter then the lemon juice and salt and pepper to taste.

Drain the trout on kitchen paper then place on a heated serving plate. Garnish with sprigs of fresh fennel and serve with the sauce.
Serves 4

FLAMING PRAWNS

500 g (1 lb) extra-
    large raw prawns,
    thawed if frozen
4 tablespoons olive
    oil
2 cloves garlic,
    crushed
½ small chilli,
    seeded and finely
    chopped
3 tablespoons
    chopped fresh
    parsley
salt
4 tablespoons brandy

Wash the prawns, remove their heads and legs and dry on kitchen paper.

Heat the oil in a large frying pan, add the garlic and chilli and cook for 1 minute. Add the prawns and cook, turning and stirring frequently, for about 3 to 4 minutes, or until they turn pink.

Sprinkle with the parsley and salt to taste. Just before serving, pour in the brandy and flame to set alight with a long taper. Serve immediately.
Serves 4

TROUT WITH SOURED CREAM

juice of 1 lemon
175 ml (6 fl oz) wine
    vinegar
salt
4 trout, cleaned with
    heads left on
50 g (2 oz) butter
284 ml (½ pint)
    carton soured
    cream
2 tablespoons snipped
    chives

Fill a large pan with just enough water to cover the fish. Add the lemon juice, wine vinegar and salt to taste. Bring to the boil, add the trout, reduce the heat to a very gentle simmer and poach for 5 to 6 minutes until the trout are cooked.

Meanwhile, melt the butter in a pan, add the soured cream and mix well. Heat very gently to warm the mixture, stirring constantly. Do not allow the mixture to boil.

Remove the trout from the poaching liquid, drain well then place on a warmed serving plate. Spoon a little of the sauce over the fish and sprinkle with the snipped chives to garnish. Serve the remaining sauce separately.
Serves 4

RED MULLET WITH LEMON AND OLIVES

4 × 250 g (8 oz) red
    mullet, cleaned and
    scaled
6 tablespoons olive
    oil
250 ml (8 fl oz) dry
    white wine
125 g (4 oz) black
    olives, pitted
2 small lemons, cut
    into wedges
2 cloves garlic, finely
    chopped
salt and pepper
3 tablespoons
    chopped parsley to
    garnish

Place the mullet in a shallow ovenproof dish. Pour over the olive oil and wine and add the olives, lemon wedges, garlic and salt and pepper to taste. Cover with foil and bake in a preheated moderate oven, 180°C (350°F), Gas Mark 4, for 20 minutes or until the fish is cooked and flakes easily when tested with the tip of a knife.

Remove from the oven, sprinkle with the parsley and serve immediately straight from the dish. Crusty Italian bread makes a good accompaniment.
Serves 4

RIGHT: *Trout with Soured Cream: Flaming Prawns; Red Mullet with Lemon and Olives.*

MEAT

The Italians take their meat seriously, be it an expensive cut of beef designed to be grilled with just a few drops of oil and sprinkling of freshly ground salt and pepper; or a long-simmered economical offal dish that relies upon careful and detailed preparation as well as the thoughtful and much considered addition of herbs, spices and stock for its success. Perhaps that is why they have so many classic meat dishes that have found world acclaim in their repetoire – dishes like Stracotto (Beef Braised in Wine), Cold Tongue Giardinera, Beef Olives, Osso Bucco (Italian Veal Stew) and Maiale al Latte (Pork Cooked in Milk).

You may choose to serve your meat dish the English way as a main course after a starter and before a pudding or dessert but for authenticity why not try it the Italian way. A formal meal in Italy is a succession of courses, with no main course, starting with an hors d'oeuvre or appetizer, followed by a first course of either pasta, risotto or soup, and a second course of meat, poultry or fish accompanied by one or two vegetable side dishes. Then there is salad, sometimes cheese, and finally the meal ends with fruit or dessert.

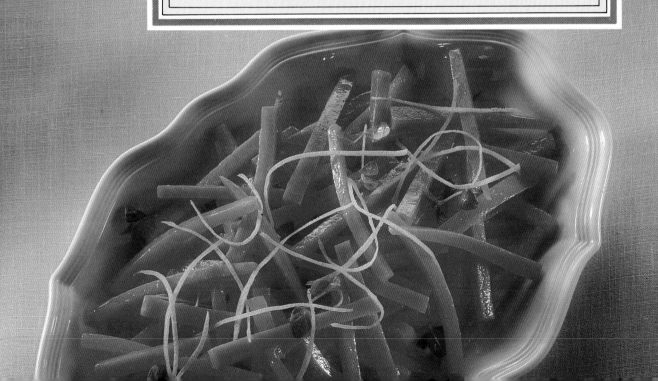

STUFFED VEAL SHOULDER

1.5 kg (3½ lb)
  shoulder of veal,
  boned
2 teaspoons lemon
  juice
salt and pepper
50 g (2 oz) butter
1 small onion,
  chopped
250 g (8 oz) pork
  sausage meat
1 tablespoon chopped
  parsley
1 egg, beaten
250 g (8 oz) frozen
  chopped spinach.
  thawed and
  squeezed dry
flour to dust
2 tablespoons olive
  oil

Sprinkle the veal with the lemon juice and season generously with salt and pepper. Fold the veal in half and sew two sides together to form a bag.

To make the stuffing, melt half of the butter in a pan, add the onion and cook for 5 minutes. Mix the onion with the sausage meat, parsley, egg, spinach and salt and pepper to taste. Stuff the veal and sew up the end.

Dust with a little flour and place in a roasting tin. Dot with the remaining butter and pour over the oil. Cover and cook in a preheated moderate oven, 160°C (325°F), Gas Mark 3, for 2-2¼ hours, turning once, or until the veal is tender and the stuffing is cooked. Remove the thread and slice the veal to serve.
Serves 6

VEAL ESCALOPES WITH HAM AND CHEESE

500 g (1 lb) veal
  fillet, cut into 4
  slices
flour for coating
salt and pepper
1 tablespoon oil
40 g (1½ oz) butter
125 g (4 oz)
Parma ham or cooked
  ham, chopped
2 tablespoons
  chopped parsley
4 tablespoons grated
  Parmesan cheese
4 tablespoons chicken
  stock

Lay the veal slices flat between greaseproof paper and beat gently to flatten. Season the flour with salt and pepper and use to coat the veal.

Heat the oil and butter in a large frying pan, add the veal and fry for about 3 minutes on each side.

Mix the ham and parsley together and spread over the veal. Sprinkle with the cheese.

Stir the stock into the pan juices and spoon a little over each portion. Cover and cook gently for 5 minutes, or until the veal is tender and the cheese melting.

Transfer to a warmed serving dish and keep hot. Bring the pan juices to the boil and cook until reduced. Pour over the veal and serve immediately.
Serves 4

BELOW: *Stuffed Veal Shoulder; Veal Escalopes with Ham and Cheese*

VEAL PARMESAN

25 g (1 oz) dry
  breadcrumbs
25 g (1 oz) grated
  Parmesan cheese
salt and pepper
500 g (1 lb) veal
  escalopes, cut into
  squares
1 egg, beaten
40 g (1½ oz) butter,
  melted
2 tablespoons olive
  oil
1 onion, thinly sliced
500 g (1 lb)
  tomatoes, skinned
  and chopped
2 tablespoons tomato
  purée
½ teaspoon sugar
½ teaspoon dried
  oregano
chopped parsley to
  garnish

Mix together the breadcrumbs, cheese and salt and pepper to taste. Dip the veal into the beaten egg, then coat with the cheese mixture.

Pour the melted butter into a baking dish and arrange the veal squares in the dish, in one layer, turning them to coat with the melted butter. Cook in a preheated moderately hot oven, 200°C (400°F), Gas Mark 6, for 20 minutes. Turn the veal and cook for 15 minutes.

Meanwhile, heat the oil in a saucepan and fry the onion until softened. Add the tomatoes, tomato purée, sugar, oregano and salt and pepper to taste and stir well. Simmer until the sauce is well reduced.

Pour the tomato sauce over the veal and heat through in the oven for 5 to 10 minutes before serving, garnished with chopped parsley.
Serves 4

VEAL WITH ORANGE

25 g (1 oz) butter
1 tablespoon oil
750 g (1½ lb)
  braising veal,
  cubed
1 onion, sliced
3 tablespoons plain
  flour
300 ml (½ pint)
  chicken stock
150 ml (¼ pint)
  fresh orange juice
salt and pepper
2 oranges, peeled and
  sliced
watercress to garnish

Melt the butter with the oil in a frying pan. Add the veal cubes and brown on all sides. Transfer with a slotted spoon to a casserole.

Add the onion to the pan and fry until golden brown. Add to the casserole.

Stir the flour into the fat remaining in the pan and cook for 3 minutes. Gradually stir in the stock and orange juice and bring to the boil. Season with salt and pepper to taste. Pour over the veal cubes. Arrange the orange slices, overlapping, on top.

Cook in a preheated moderate oven, 180°C (350°F), Gas Mark 4, for 1½ to 2 hours or until the veal is tender. Garnish with watercress.
Serves 4

VEAL OLIVES WITH MUSHROOMS

12 small veal
  escalopes
6 slices of cooked ham
12 spring onions
125 g (4 oz) mature
  Cheddar cheese,
  cut into 12 sticks
  about 5 mm (¼
  inch) wide
75 g (3 oz) butter
250 g (8 oz) button
  mushrooms, sliced
150 ml (¼ pint) dry
  white wine
salt and pepper
watercress to garnish

Put the escalopes between sheets of greaseproof paper and beat until thin. Cut each slice of ham in half. Place a half ham slice, a spring onion and a stick of cheese on each veal escalope and roll up. Tie with string or secure with wooden cocktail sticks.

Melt the butter in a large frying pan. Add the veal rolls and brown on all sides; remove from the pan as they brown.

Add the mushrooms to the pan and fry for 5 minutes. Stir in the wine with salt and pepper to taste and bring to the boil. Return the veal rolls to the pan and simmer, covered, for about 10 minutes or until tender. Serve garnished with watercress.
Serves 6

RIGHT: *Veal Olives with Mushrooms*

PAPRIKA LAMB

4 lamb chops
1 onion, finely
    chopped
150 g (5 oz) carton
    natural low-fat
    yogurt
2 teaspoons paprika
MARINADE:
2 tablespoons white
    wine
2 teaspoons lemon
    juice
½ teaspoon sugar
½ teaspoon dried
    thyme
salt and pepper
TO GARNISH:
paprika
parsley sprigs

Mix together the marinade ingredients, with salt and pepper to taste. Trim the chops and remove any excess fat. Place in the marinade and leave for 2 to 3 hours.

Drain the chops and dry with kitchen paper. Place them in a shallow ovenproof dish. Sprinkle the onion over the chops and cover with foil. Cook in a preheated moderately hot oven, 190°C (375°F), Gas Mark 5, for 1 hour.

Mix the yogurt with the paprika and spoon over the chops. Continue cooking for a further 15 minutes. Serve sprinkled with paprika and garnished with parsley.
Serves 4

ITALIAN SALAMI PLATTER

500 g (1 lb) mixed
    Italian cured or
    preserved meats
    (for example,
    Italian salami,
    Parma ham,
    Mortadella
    sausage, Italian
    garlic sausage,
    cooked tongue or
    bresaola) thinly
    sliced
TO SERVE:
figs, olives, sun-dried
    tomatoes, pickles
    or radishes

Arrange the chosen selection of cured and preserved meats on a large serving platter. Garnish with figs, olives, sun-dried tomatoes, pickles or radishes.

Serve with bread and a selection of salads.
Serves 6 to 8

ROMAN PORK CASSEROLE

25 g (1 oz) plain
    flour
salt and pepper
1 kg (2 lb) pork
    fillet, cubed
25 g (1 oz) butter
1 tablespoon olive oil
250 g (8 oz)
    mushrooms, sliced
1 clove garlic, crushed
1 × 397 g (14 oz)
    can chopped
    tomatoes, drained
150 ml (¼ pint)
    Marsala
1 teaspoon dried basil
½ teaspoon dried
    oregano
chopped parsley to
    garnish

Season the flour and use to coat the pork fillet. Melt the butter with the oil in a flameproof casserole. Add the pork fillet and brown on all sides, then remove and set aside.

Add the mushrooms and garlic to the casserole and fry for 3 minutes. Stir in the tomatoes, Marsala, herbs and seasoning to taste. Bring to the boil.

Return the pork to the casserole and mix into the sauce. Cover and cook in a preheated moderate oven, 160°C (325°F), Gas Mark 3, for 45 minutes. Serve garnished with parsley.
Serves 4

ROMAN-STYLE BEEF STEW

40 g (1½ oz) lard
1 small onion, finely
  chopped
25 g (1 oz) ham or
  bacon fat, finely
  chopped
1 celery stick, diced
1 clove garlic, sliced
750 g (1½ lb)
  stewing beef, cut
  into 2.5 cm (1
  inch) cubes
¼ teaspoon dried
  marjoram
salt and pepper
200 ml (7 fl oz)
  full-bodied red
  wine
300-450 ml (½-¾
  pint) beef stock
1 tablespoon tomato
  purée
TO SERVE:
1 head celery,
  trimmed and cut
  into 5 cm (2 inch)
  lengths

Melt the lard in a heavy pan, add the onion and fry gently until transparent. Add the ham or bacon fat, celery and garlic and cook for 1 minute. Add the meat, marjoram, and salt and pepper to taste. Cook, stirring frequently, for 2 minutes.

Add the wine, bring to the boil and simmer until reduced by half. Add 300 ml (½ pint) of the stock and the tomato purée. Cover and cook very gently for 3 to 4 hours, until the meat is tender and the sauce is thick and rich. Stir occasionally and add the remaining stock a little at a time during cooking if the sauce reduces too quickly.

Meanwhile, cook the celery in boiling salted water for 15 to 20 minutes until tender. Drain and add to the stew just before serving, or serve separately.
Serves 4

ROLLED VEAL SKEWERS

4 veal escalopes
4 thin slices Parma
  ham
1 small green pepper,
  cored and seeded
1 tablespoon mild
  English mustard
24 stuffed green
  olives
MARINADE:
4 tablespoons olive
  oil
2 tablespoons lemon
  juice
1 clove garlic, crushed
1 tablespoon mixed
  herbs
salt and pepper

Place the veal escalopes between two sheets of dampened greaseproof paper and beat out until very thin. Divide each escalope into four pieces. Cut each slice of ham into four pieces and cut the pepper into 12 pieces.

Spread each portion of veal with mustard, top with a slice of ham and roll up with the ham inside. Thread the veal rolls onto four skewers alternating with the pieces of pepper and olives. Place in a dish.

Beat the oil with the lemon juice, garlic, herbs and salt and pepper to taste. Pour over the kebabs, cover and leave to marinate for 1-2 hours, turning them occasionally.

Remove the kebabs from the marinade and cook under a moderate grill, or over a charcoal grill, for 10-15 minutes, basting frequently with the marinade during cooking.
Serves 4

┌─────────────────────────────┐
│ **MARINADES** │
└─────────────────────────────┘

The Italians know that a marinade can make all the difference between an ordinary meal and an unforgettable one. A marinade flavours meat and sometimes tenderizes it before cooking. Marinate in a tightly covered dish or use a large plastic bag and simply turn the bag to redistribute the marinade. Marinate for several hours in the refrigerator or for at least an hour or two if in a hurry. The marinade used in Rolled Veal Skewers (this page) can also be used to marinade poultry, steaks, spareribs, chops and roasts.

ITALIAN SHERRIED VEAL

4 veal steaks
25 g (1 oz) butter
1 small onion, finely
  chopped
4½ tablespoons dry
  sherry
2 teaspoons plain
  flour
125 ml (4 fl oz)
  water
½ beef stock cube
125 g (4 oz)
  mushrooms, sliced
salt and pepper
2 tablespoons
  chopped parsley
2 tablespoons double
  cream

Beat the veal steaks between sheets of greaseproof paper until thin.

Melt the butter in a large heavy-based frying pan, add the veal steaks and cook quickly on both sides to brown, about 3-4 minutes. Remove with a slotted spoon and set aside.

Add the onion to the pan juices and cook for 2 minutes. Add the sherry, bring to the boil and cook for 15 seconds. Stir in the flour, mixing well then add the water with the stock cube and mix to blend to a smooth sauce. Bring to the boil, reduce the heat, add the veal steaks, mushrooms and salt and pepper to taste. Cover and simmer gently for 6-8 minutes.

Stir in the parsley and cream, mixing well. Cook for 1 minute to reheat then serve at once.
Serves 4

LEFT: *Paprika Lamb*

CREAMED KIDNEYS WITH SALAMI

4-5 lambs' kidneys
15 g (½ oz) butter
1 small onion,
  chopped
25 g (1 oz)
  mushrooms,
  chopped
2 teaspoons plain
  flour
150 ml (¼ pint)
  stock
1-2 tablespoons
  raisins
2 slices salami,
  chopped
salt and pepper
2 tablespoons single
  cream

Remove the skin and core from the kidneys and chop. Melt the butter in a heavy-based pan. Add the onion and fry until soft. Add the kidneys and mushrooms and cook for 2 to 3 minutes. Stir in the flour and cook for 1 minute. Gradually blend in the stock and heat, stirring, until thickened.

Add the raisins, salami and salt and pepper to taste. Cover and simmer for 15 minutes.

Remove from the heat, stir in the cream and serve immediately, with boiled rice.

Serves 2

VEAL ROMAN STYLE

8 slices bacon
8 veal escalopes,
  weighing about
  75 g (3 oz) each
8 sprigs of fresh sage
50 g (2 oz) butter
7 tablespoons dry
  white wine
salt and pepper
fresh sage leaves, to
  garnish

Place a slice of the bacon on top of each slice of veal then add a sprig of sage. Secure together with wooden cocktail sticks. Melt the butter in a frying pan until foaming. Add the veal slices and fry until browned on both sides, about 2-3 minutes.

Add the wine and salt and pepper to taste. Simmer gently for about 6-8 minutes, or until the meat is tender.

Remove the veal slices with a slotted spoon and place on a heated serving dish. Remove and discard the cocktail sticks. Add 1 tablespoon of water to the pan juices and mix well. Simmer for 1 minute then pour over the veal slices. Garnish with sage.

Serves 4

VEAL

Veal features in many Italian dishes. It is a meat with little fat and without a strong flavour of its own; consequently it needs careful cooking and additional seasoning in the way of stuffings and sauces. Good quality veal is soft and finely grained and varies in colour from off-white to pale pink. What may seem like a large amount of gelatinous tissue is a normal characteristic of the meat and nothing to worry about. It usually softens and shrinks when cooked.

ROAST STUFFED SHOULDER OF VEAL

1 × 1.25 kg (2½ lb) boned shoulder of veal
25 g (1 oz) fresh breadcrumbs
1 teaspoon dried sage
2 tablespoons chopped parsley
1 clove garlic, crushed
3 tablespoons double cream
1 egg yolk
salt and pepper
1 onion, sliced
6 carrots, sliced
1 bay leaf
125 ml (4 fl oz) dry white wine
125 ml (4 fl oz) water
3-4 tablespoons tomato purée
parsley sprigs to garnish

Lay the veal flat on a working surface. Mix together the breadcrumbs, herbs, garlic, cream, egg yolk, salt and pepper. Spread over the veal, then roll up and tie securely into shape. Rub with salt and pepper and place, join side down, in a roasting tin. Arrange the onion, carrots and bay leaf around the veal.

Roast in a preheated moderately hot oven, 200°C (400°F), Gas Mark 6, for 30 minutes. Turn the veal join side up and continue roasting for 30 minutes.

Turn the veal join side down again. Mix together the wine, water and tomato purée and pour over the meat. Continue roasting, basting frequently, for 1 hour or until the veal is cooked through. If the veal seems to be browning too quickly, cover with foil.

Transfer the veal to a warmed serving dish and garnish with parsley sprigs. Strain the cooking liquid and serve as a sauce.
Serves 6

STEWED LAMB WITH TOMATOES

4 tablespoons oil
1.25-1.5 kg (3-3½ lb) stewing lamb, cubed
2 onions, sliced
1 × 397 g (14 oz) can chopped tomatoes
4 tablespoons tomato purée
600 ml (1 pint) beef stock
1 clove garlic, crushed
1 teaspoon each dried basil and marjoram
1 bay leaf
salt and pepper
1 tablespoon cornflour, blended with 2 tablespoons water

Heat the oil in a pan and brown the lamb, a few pieces at a time, transferring the pieces to a large casserole as they brown. Add the onions to the pan and cook until soft. Stir in the remaining ingredients, except the blended cornflour mixture, with salt and pepper to taste. Bring to the boil, then pour over the lamb. Cover and cook in a preheated cool oven, 150°C (300°F), Gas Mark 2, for 3 hours.

Remove the lamb with a slotted spoon and reserve. Allow the sauce to cool then skim off the fat. Add the reserved lamb and bring to the boil. Stir in the blended cornflour and simmer, stirring, for 2 to 3 minutes until thickened. Check the seasoning. Serve with tagliatelle.
Serves 4

LEFT: *Veal Roman Style*

RIGHT: *Roast Stuffed Shoulder of Veal*

VEAL WITH TUNA FISH MAYONNAISE

1 kg (2 lb) piece
    boned and rolled
    shoulder of veal
1 carrot, halved
1 onion, halved
1 celery stick, sliced
1 bay leaf
4 peppercorns
1 teaspoon salt
300 ml (½ pint)
    Tuna Fish
    Mayonnaise (see
    page 152)
TO GARNISH:
strips of anchovy
    fillets
drained capers
few black olives
thin lemon slices

Put the meat into a saucepan just large enough to hold it. Add the carrot, onion, celery, bay leaf, peppercorns and 1 teaspoon salt. Add just enough water to cover and bring slowly to the boil. Skim the surface, cover and simmer for 1½ to 2 hours, until tender. Leave in the stock until cold.

Drain the meat and carve into neat slices. Lightly cover the base of a serving dish with half of the Tuna Fish Mayonnaise and arrange the meat on top. Spoon over the remaining dressing to cover the meat completely.

Cover the dish loosely with foil and leave in the refrigerator overnight.

Garnish with anchovies, capers, olives and lemon slices.

Serves 4 to 6

AUBERGINE AND BACON CASSEROLE

750 g (1½ lb)
    aubergines, cut
    into 1 cm (½ inch)
    slices
salt and pepper
5 tablespoons oil
    (approximately)
250 g (8 oz) streaky
    bacon rashers,
    derinded and diced
1 large onion,
    chopped
1 clove garlic, crushed
1 medium green
    pepper, cored,
    deseeded and diced
250 g (8 oz)
    mushrooms, sliced
1 × 397 g (14 oz)
    can chopped
    tomatoes
½ teaspoon dried
    thyme
1 teaspoon sugar
125 g (4 oz)
    Mozzarella or
    Gruyère cheese,
    grated

Sprinkle the aubergine slices with salt and leave to drain for 30 minutes. Rinse and pat dry.

Brush a baking sheet with a little of the oil and arrange the aubergine slices on top in a single layer. Brush with the remaining oil. Cook in a preheated hot oven, 230°C (450°F), Gas Mark 8, for 35 minutes.

Meanwhile, fry the bacon in a frying pan until crisp, then remove.

Add the onion, garlic and green pepper to the pan and fry until the onion is softened. Stir in the mushrooms, tomatoes, with their juice, thyme, salt and pepper to taste and the sugar. Simmer until quite thick, stirring occasionally.

Layer the aubergine slices, bacon and tomato sauce in a shallow casserole. Top with the cheese.

Reduce the oven temperature to moderate, 180°C (350°F), Gas Mark 4, and cook for 20 minutes or until beginning to brown.

Serves 4 to 6

ABOVE: *Veal with Tuna Fish Mayonnaise*

RIGHT: *Pork Cooked in Milk*

GAMMON WITH BEANS AND TOMATOES

500-750 g (1-1½ lb)
  smoked boneless
  gammon joint
125 g (4 oz) dried
  haricot beans,
  soaked in cold
  water for 4 hours
1 onion, chopped
1 clove garlic, crushed
400 g (14 oz) can
  peeled tomatoes
1 tablespoon chopped
  parsley
salt and pepper

Place the gammon in a pan and cover with cold water. Bring to the boil, reduce the heat and cook for 10 minutes.

Add the beans, onion, garlic, tomatoes and their juice, parsley and salt and pepper to taste. Cover and simmer gently for 1-1½ hours until the gammon and beans are tender and cooked.

Remove the gammon and cut into slices. Serve the gammon slices with the bean and tomato sauce and mashed potato or pasta, if liked.
Serves 4

PORK COOKED IN MILK

1 tablespoon oil
25 g (1 oz) butter
1 clove garlic
1 rosemary sprig
1 kg (2 lb) piece
  boned and rolled
  loin of pork,
  derinded and
  secured with string
salt and pepper
600 ml (1 pint) milk

Heat the oil and butter with the garlic and rosemary in a flameproof casserole just large enough to hold the meat. Add the meat and fry, turning, until well browned all over. Season with salt and pepper to taste. Discard the garlic and rosemary.

Put the milk in a pan and bring to simmering point. Pour over the pork and cover, leaving the lid slightly tilted. Simmer for about 2 hours, turning occasionally, until the meat is tender and the milk reduced to about 150 ml (¼ pint).

Carve the meat into fairly thick slices, arrange on a warmed serving dish and keep hot. Skim off any surface fat from the milk, then stir, scraping the base of the pan to incorporate the meat residue. Reheat and spoon over the meat.
Serves 5 to 6

ROAST LAMB WITH ROSEMARY

1 × 1.5 kg (3½ lb) leg of lamb
2-4 cloves garlic, sliced
3-4 rosemary sprigs
salt and pepper
1 tablespoon oil
150 ml (¼ pint) dry white wine or light stock

Make small incisions in the lamb and insert a piece of garlic and a few rosemary leaves into each. Season with salt and pepper and place on a rack in a roasting tin. Spoon over the oil.

Cook in a preheated moderate oven, 180°C (350°F), Gas Mark 4, for about 2 hours. Transfer to a warmed serving dish and keep hot.

Skim the fat from the pan juices, add the wine or stock and bring to the boil, stirring, until thickened. Strain into a sauce boat and serve with the meat.

Serves 6

PIQUANT LAMB CHOPS

8 lamb chops
4 tablespoons olive oil
2 cloves garlic, chopped
2 teaspoons chopped marjoram
2 tablespoons chopped parsley
1½ tablespoons capers, drained and chopped
salt and pepper
1 tablespoon lemon juice
TO GARNISH:
sauté potatoes
lemon wedges

Lay the chops side by side in a dish, spoon the oil over them and sprinkle with the garlic. Cover and marinate for 2 hours, turning once.

Strain the marinade into a large frying pan, add the herbs and capers and heat gently. Add the chops and fry for 5 minutes on each side. Season with salt and pepper to taste, sprinkle with the lemon juice and cook, covered, over a low heat for 5 minutes.

Pile the potatoes on a warmed serving dish and arrange the chops around the edge. Spoon some of the pan juices over the chops and garnish the dish with lemon wedges.

Serves 4

SPRING LAMB IN LEMON SAUCE

750 g (1½ lb) boned shoulder or leg of lamb
25 g (1 oz) lard
50 g (2 oz) unsmoked gammon, chopped
1 onion, chopped
2 tablespoons plain flour
salt and pepper
4 tablespoons dry white wine or Vermouth
300 ml (½ pint) light stock
2 egg yolks
2 tablespoons lemon juice
½ teaspoon finely grated lemon rind
1 teaspoon chopped marjoram
1 tablespoon chopped parsley

Cut the lamb into 2.5 cm (1 inch) cubes. Melt the lard in a heavy pan, add the gammon, lamb and onion and fry gently for 10 minutes, stirring frequently. Sprinkle in the flour and season to taste with salt and pepper. Cook, stirring, for 1 minute.

Add the wine or Vermouth, bring to the boil and boil until reduced by half. Add the stock and bring back to the boil, stirring. Cover and simmer for 45 minutes, or until the lamb is tender. Skim off any surface fat.

Beat together the egg yolks, lemon juice and rind, and herbs. Add 3 tablespoons of the cooking liquor and blend well. Add to the pan and stir just until the sauce thickens; do not allow to boil. Check the seasoning and serve with ribbon noodles or new potatoes.

Serves 4

Spring Lamb in Lemon Sauce; Roast Lamb with Rosemary; Piquant Lamb Chops

BEEF OLIVES

1 kg (2 lb) piece of beef top rump, cut into 6 slices
salt and pepper
1 teaspoon dried thyme
12 thin slices of smoked ham
25 g (1 oz) butter
1 tablespoon oil
1 onion, chopped
300 ml (½ pint) stout
thyme sprigs to garnish (optional)

Pound the beef slices until they are thin, then cut each slice in half to make 12 slices, each about 13 × 9 cm (5 × 3½ inches). Rub each slice with a little seasoning and thyme, then place a slice of ham on each and trim to fit; reserve any trimmings. Roll up and secure with string.

Melt the butter with the oil in a flameproof casserole. Add the beef rolls and brown on all sides. Remove and set aside.

Add the onion to the casserole with any ham trimmings and fry until softened. Return the beef rolls to the casserole and pour over the stout. Bring to the boil, then cover and transfer to a preheated moderate oven, 180°C (350°F), Gas Mark 4. Cook for 1 hour or until the beef rolls are tender. Remove the string. Garnish with thyme sprigs and serve with carrots, if liked.

Serves 4 to 6

ROAST LEG OF LAMB PARMA

250 g (8 oz) frozen chopped spinach, thawed
ground mace
salt and pepper
5 slices Parma or other smoked ham, halved crossways
2.25-2.5 kg (5-5½ lb) leg of lamb
2 tablespoons oil
10 small potatoes
5 onions, halved
450 ml (¾ pint) dry white wine
1 × 400 g (13 oz) can artichoke hearts, drained
chopped parsley to garnish

Squeeze the spinach until dry, then mix in mace, salt and pepper to taste. Put a portion on each piece of ham and roll into small cylinders.

Make 10 deep slashes at regular intervals in the lamb and insert the ham. Sprinkle with salt and pepper.

Heat the oil in a roasting tin, add the meat and baste. Cook in a pre-heated moderately hot oven, 200°C (400°F), Gas Mark 6, allowing 20 minutes per 500 g (1 lb) plus 15 minutes. Add the potatoes and onions to the tin for the last hour; season and baste well.

Transfer the lamb and vegetables to a large dish. Keep hot.

Drain off the fat from the pan, pour in the wine and heat gently, stirring to incorporate the sediment in the tin. Add the artichokes and heat through for about 3 minutes. Sprinkle the potatoes with parsley; serve the sauce separately.

Serves 10

SOURED CREAM

Soured cream isn't cream that has gone sour but is cultured fresh cream with a pleasant acidic flavour and smooth texture. Cultured soured cream will not freeze nor will it whip. If soured cream is unavailable then it is possible to make a good substitute by mixing 142 ml (¼ pint) carton double cream with 2-3 teaspoons lemon juice.

LEFT: *Roast Leg of Lamb Parma*

RIGHT: *Cold Tongue Giardinera*

COLD TONGUE GIARDINERA

125 g (4 oz) frozen mixed vegetables, lightly cooked
2 pickled onions, chopped
2 gherkins, chopped
6 stuffed olives, sliced
50 g (2 oz) capers, chopped
4 tablespoons French dressing
1 tablespoon vinegar (from the pickles)
375 g (12 oz) cooked tongue, thinly sliced
4 hard-boiled eggs, sliced
chopped parsley to garnish

Put the vegetables in a bowl with the pickled onions, gherkins, olives, capers, French dressing and pickling vinegar. Leave to marinate for 4 hours.

Arrange the tongue slices on a serving dish and spoon over the vegetable mixture. Garnish with egg slices and parsley. Serve cold, with crusty bread rolls.

Serves 4

ITALIAN BEEF BAKE

175 g (6 oz) macaroni
500 g (1 lb) mince
1 onion, chopped
2-3 cloves garlic, crushed
2 sticks celery, sliced
397 g (14 oz) can chopped tomatoes
3 tablespoons ketchup
2 teaspoons herbs
150 ml (¼ pint) stock
1 tablespoon cornflour
2 courgettes, chopped
SAUCE:
25 g (1 oz) flour
25 g (1 oz) margarine
300 ml (½ pint) milk
50 g (2 oz) skimmed milk soft cheese
1 tablespoon dry breadcrumbs

Cook the pasta according to the packet instructions, then drain. Dry-fry the beef until browned. Add the onion, garlic and celery and cook until soft. Add the tomatoes, ketchup, herbs, stock and cornflour dissolved in 2 tablespoons water. Bring to the boil, reduce heat and simmer, uncovered, for 15 minutes.

Add the courgettes and simmer for a further 5 minutes until thickened. Add the pasta, mix well and place in a large shallow ovenproof dish.

To make the sauce, place the flour, margarine and milk in a pan. Bring to the boil, whisking until smooth and thickened. Add the cheese and mix. Pour over the pasta mixture.

Sprinkle with the breadcrumbs. Bake in a preheated oven, 180°C (350°F), Gas Mark 4, for 20 minutes.

Serves 4

BEEF BRAISED IN WINE

1 tablespoon oil
25 g (1 oz) butter
1 small onion, chopped
1 small carrot, chopped
1 celery stick, chopped
1.5 kg (3½ lb) piece beef topside, boned aitchbone or top rump
200 ml (7 fl oz) full-bodied red wine
200 ml (7 fl oz) beef stock
1 tablespoon tomato purée
1 thyme sprig
1 bay leaf
salt and pepper

Heat the oil and butter in a flameproof casserole, add the onion, carrot and celery and fry gently for 5 minutes, stirring occasionally.

Increase the heat, add the meat and cook, turning, until sealed. Add the wine, bring to the boil and simmer until well reduced.

Add the stock, tomato purée, herbs, and salt and pepper to taste. Bring to simmering point, cover and cook in a preheated cool oven, 150°C (300°F), Gas Mark 2, for 3 hours or until tender.

Slice the meat thickly, arrange on a warmed serving dish and keep hot.

Discard the herbs. If necessary, reduce the sauce to about 150 ml (¼ pint) by boiling uncovered, stirring frequently. Check the seasoning and spoon over the meat.

Serves 8

Meatballs in Tomato Sauce

APOLLO STEAKS

2 tablespoons oil
4 sirloin steaks, about
  1-2 cm (½-¾
  inch) thick
SAUCE:
25 g (1 oz) butter or
  margarine
1 lamb's kidney,
  skinned, cored and
  chopped
1 large onion, sliced
2 tomatoes, skinned
  and chopped
1 green pepper,
  cored, seeded and
  chopped
125 ml (4 fl oz) rosé
  wine or stock
salt and pepper

To make the sauce, melt the butter in a pan, add the kidney, onion, tomatoes and green pepper and cook until just tender, about 8 minutes.

Heat the oil in a shallow frying pan until hot, add the steaks and fry over a high heat, on both sides, for about 1 minute. Reduce the heat and cook according to how you like your steak – allow a further 4 minutes for rare; 5-6 minutes for medium; and 7-9 minutes for well done.

Meanwhile, add the wine or stock to the kidney mixture with salt and pepper to taste and cook until slightly reduced.

Transfer the steaks to warmed serving plates and serve coated with the sauce.
Serves 4

MEATBALLS IN TOMATO SAUCE

MEATBALLS:
500 g (1 lb) lean
  minced beef
1 clove garlic, crushed
1 tablespoon chopped
  parsley
½ teaspoon cumin
  seeds (optional)
salt and pepper
1 egg, beaten
SAUCE:
2 onions, finely
  chopped
1 × 397 g (14 oz)
  can chopped
  tomatoes
1 tablespoon tomato
  purée
½ teaspoon sugar
grated nutmeg
TO GARNISH:
chopped parsley

Put the beef, garlic, parsley, cumin seeds (if using) and salt and pepper to taste in a bowl; mix well. Bind the mixture with the egg, then divide into 20 and shape into balls on a floured surface.

Place the sauce ingredients, with nutmeg, salt and pepper to taste, in a large flameproof casserole. Bring to the boil, then lower the heat. Carefully place the meatballs in the liquid, cover and simmer gently for 40 to 45 minutes, stirring occasionally.

Transfer the meatballs to a hot serving dish and pour the sauce over. Serve garnished with chopped parsley.
Serves 4

SWEETBREADS WITH PEAS

500 g (1 lb) lambs'
  sweetbreads
1 tablespoon vinegar
2 tablespoons oil
40 g (1½ oz) butter
2-3 sage sprigs,
  bruised
75 g (3 oz) smoked
  streaky bacon,
  derinded and diced
6 tablespoons
  Marsala
1 teaspoon lemon
  juice
salt and pepper
250 g (8 oz) shelled
  peas, cooked and
  drained

Soak the sweetbreads in cold water for 1 hour. Drain, cover with fresh water and add the vinegar. Bring to the boil and simmer for 5 minutes.

Drain and peel any membranes from the sweetbreads, then cut into 2.5 cm (1 inch) pieces.

Heat the oil and butter in a pan, add the sage, bacon and sweetbreads and cook over moderate heat, stirring frequently, for 5 minutes. Add half the Marsala and cook for about 5 minutes, until almost evaporated.

Add the remaining Marsala, the lemon juice, and salt and pepper to taste. Simmer until reduced and thickened. Discard the sage, stir in the peas and serve immediately, with noodles.
Serves 4

ITALIAN POT ROAST

1-1.25 kg (2-3 lb)
    piece of beef topside
salt and pepper
3 tablespoons olive
    oil
1 onion, chopped
1 clove garlic, crushed
2 large carrots, sliced
2 celery sticks, sliced
1 × 230 g (8 oz) can
    chopped tomatoes
300 ml (½ pint) dry
    red wine
1 teaspoon dried
    oregano
1 bay leaf

Rub the beef all over with salt and pepper. Heat the oil in a flameproof casserole, add the beef and brown on all sides, then remove from the casserole.

Add the onion, garlic, carrots and celery to the casserole and fry until the onion is softened. Stir in the tomatoes, wine, oregano and bay leaf and bring to the boil.

Return the beef to the casserole and turn over in the liquid. Cover tightly and cook in a preheated moderate oven, 180°C (350°F), Gas Mark 4, for 3 hours or until the meat is tender. Baste occasionally during the cooking.

Remove the beef from the casserole, place on a warmed serving plate and keep hot.

Boil the cooking liquid on top of the stove until well reduced and thickened. Strain and serve as a sauce, with the beef.

Serves 4

ITALIAN BEEF CASSEROLE

2 tablespoons olive
    oil
1 onion, chopped
1 clove garlic, crushed
4 bacon rashers,
    derinded and diced
2 carrots, diced
1 celery stick, diced
500 g (1 lb) minced
    beef
1 × 295 g (10 oz)
    can condensed
    tomato soup
1 × 397 g (14 oz)
    can tomatoes,
    drained
1 teaspoon dried basil
salt and pepper
250 g (8 oz)
    tagliatelle
125 g (4 oz)
    Cheddar cheese,
    grated

Heat the oil in a frying pan, add the onion, garlic and bacon and fry until the onion is softened. Add the carrots and celery and continue frying for 3 minutes. Stir in the beef and brown well, then add the soup, tomatoes, basil and salt and pepper to taste. Cook gently for about 15 minutes.

Meanwhile, cook the noodles in boiling salted water until tender. Drain well. Add the noodles to the beef mixture and fold together, then turn into a casserole. Sprinkle the cheese over the top. Cook in a preheated moderate oven, 180°C (350°F), Gas Mark 4, for 30 minutes.

Serves 4

Italian Pot Roast; Italian Beef Casserole

POULTRY AND GAME

The many and varied recipes from the various regions of Italy can provide the adventurous as well as the novice cook with a wide and enticing repertoire when cooking poultry and game. Some recipes are seemingly simple affairs of grilled or barbecued chicken, duck or game birds, but most have usually been marinated in a spicy, herby or lemony mixture for several hours, which imparts a delicious and unique flavour to the most humble of birds.

Other recipes combine poultry and game with cured meats and ham, making a rich but succulent dish that scores high on flavour and originality; yet others rely upon time-honoured slow-cooking methods of baking, stewing and poaching that can lift a homely casserole into a dinner party delight.

Regional favourites include stuffing poultry and game birds with herb-flavoured cheeses, roasting pigeons in a herb and lemon-flavoured butter, and sautéeing, then flaming chicken livers with Marsala. All make a welcome and nutritious main course for a truly memorable Italian meal.

Turkey Fillets with Tuna

POUSSINS MEDICI

2 poussins, halved
    lengthways
50 g (2 oz) butter
1 tablespoon oil
4 rosemary sprigs
150 ml (¼ pint) red
    wine or port
142 ml (¼ pint)
    carton single cream
salt and pepper
rosemary sprigs to
    garnish (optional)

Flatten each poussin half slightly. Heat the butter and oil in a large pan, add the rosemary and poussins, skin side down, and fry gently for 8 to 10 minutes or until golden. Turn and cook the other side for 8 to 10 minutes. Transfer the poussins to a warmed serving dish keep warm.

Add the wine to the pan, stirring well to scrape up the sediment. Simmer, uncovered, until reduced by half. Add the cream, and salt and pepper to taste, tilting the pan to mix, and continue cooking until a smooth sauce forms. Remove the rosemary.

Pour the sauce over the poussins and garnish with rosemary sprigs if liked. Serve with mange tout.
Serves 2 to 4

TURKEY FILLETS WITH TUNA

4 × 125 g (4 oz)
    turkey breast fillets
salt and pepper
25 g (1 oz) butter
1 tablespoon olive oil
6 tablespoons medium
    dry white wine
1 × 198 g (7 oz) can
    tuna fish, drained
2 teaspoons tomato
    purée
150 g (5 oz) carton
    natural yogurt
TO GARNISH:
2 tablespoons
    chopped parsley
12 black olives
4 lemon wedges

Sprinkle the turkey fillets with salt and pepper to taste. Heat the butter and oil in a heavy-based frying pan, add the turkey and fry gently for 3 to 4 minutes on each side, until well browned. Add the wine and cook gently for 2 to 3 minutes. Transfer the turkey to a warmed serving dish and keep hot.

Mash the tuna fish, tomato purée and a little of the yogurt together to form a creamy paste, then fold in the remaining yogurt. Pour into the pan, stirring well to blend, and heat through quickly. Spoon over the turkey, sprinkle with the parsley and garnish with the olives and lemon wedges.

Serve with tagliatelle verdi.
Serves 4

ITALIAN ORANGE CHICKEN

1 small chicken
1 onion, halved
250 g (8 oz) carrots,
    peeled
1 clove garlic, crushed
3 tablespoons olive
    oil
1 large red
    pepper, cored and
    seeded
few drops of chilli
    sauce
2 tablespoons fresh
    tomato sauce
2 oranges, peeled and
    segmented
2 tablespoons
    chopped mixed
    fresh herbs
salt and pepper

Remove all the flesh from the chicken and cut into bite-sized pieces. Place all the chicken bones in a pan, add water to cover, one half of the onion and the carrots. Bring to the boil, reduce the heat and simmer for 15-20 minutes. Remove the carrots and continue to cook the stock if necessary until reduced by half.

Meanwhile, slice the remaining onion. Heat the oil in a large casserole or pan and add the onion. Cook gently with the garlic until tender, about 5 minutes. Cut the pepper into eighths, add to the onion mixture and cook for 3 minutes. Add the chilli sauce, tomato sauce, the chicken and 300 ml (½ pint) of the prepared stock. Bring to the boil, reduce the heat and simmer for 10 minutes.

Slice the carrots and add to the chicken with the orange segments, herbs and salt and pepper to taste. Simmer for a further 5 minutes.
Serves 4

QUAILS BIANCO

125 g (4 oz) butter
8 quails
pepper
4 slices Parma or
  other raw smoked
  ham, halved
  crossways
10 fresh or preserved
  vine leaves,
  blanched
3 fresh figs, quartered
4 tablespoons rosé
  wine
150 ml (¼ pint)
  white Vermouth

Spread half the butter all over the quails, then sprinkle with pepper. Wrap a half slice of ham over the breast of each quail, securing underneath with a wooden cocktail stick. Place each quail on a vine leaf. Shred the 2 remaining leaves.

Generously coat the inside of a shallow ovenproof dish with the remaining butter. Place the quails, on the leaves, in the dish, arranging the shredded leaves and the fig segments near the centre. Pour over the wine and Vermouth. Cook in a preheated moderate oven, 180°C (350°F), Gas Mark 4, for 40 to 45 minutes, basting occasionally.

Serve with a julienne of celery, courgette and carrot.

Serves 4

ROAST PIGEONS PALOMA

50 g (2 oz) butter,
  softened
1 teaspoon chopped
  parsley
1 teaspoon chopped
  lemon balm
  (optional)
1 teaspoon chopped
  chives
½ teaspoon of Tabasco
2 oven-ready wood
  pigeons
2 × 8 cm (3 inch)
  wide sheets pork
  barding fat, thinly
  sliced
1 teaspoon plain flour
1 tablespoon lemon
  juice
TO GARNISH:
lemon balm or
  parsley
small bunch of grapes

Blend the butter with the herbs and Tabasco and put half the mixture inside the body cavity of each pigeon. Wrap each pigeon in a piece of pork fat and truss, bringing the trussing strings across the breast to secure firmly.

Place the pigeons in a roasting tin and cook in a preheated moderately hot oven, 200°C (400°F), Gas Mark 6, for 20 to 25 minutes, basting twice.

Remove the barding fat, sprinkle the breasts with the flour, baste again and return to the oven for 5 minutes, until golden. Pour the lemon juice into the pan, stirring to dissolve the sediment, then spoon over the pigeons.

Transfer to a warmed serving dish and garnish with lemon balm or parsley and grapes. Serve with game chips (see box tip page 68).

Serves 2

POUSSINS DIABOLO

125 g (4 oz) butter,
  softened
½ teaspoon dry
  mustard
pinch of chilli powder
1 teaspoon anchovy
  essence or sauce
1 teaspoon Worcester-
  shire sauce
½ teaspoon celery
  salt
4 poussins
4 teaspoons capers
watercress sprigs to
  garnish

Place the butter in a small bowl, add all the seasonings and beat until well blended. Spread all over the poussins and inside the cavities. Put a teaspoon of capers inside each poussin.

Place in a roasting tin and cook in a preheated moderately hot oven, 190°C (375°F), Gas Mark 5, for 40 to 45 minutes, basting occasionally, until golden brown.

Transfer to a warmed serving dish and garnish with watercress. Serve with toast spread with a parsley-flavoured butter, steamed potatoes, and a watercress and radish salad.

Serves 4

Poussins Diabolo

CHICKEN WITH AUBERGINES AND COURGETTES

1 aubergine, sliced
1 teaspoon salt
1 × 1.5 kg (3½ lb) chicken
1 onion, sliced
2 cloves garlic, crushed
3 courgettes, sliced
4 tomatoes, skinned and chopped
2 tablespoons tomato purée
300 ml (½ pint) chicken stock
1½ teaspoons cumin seeds
½ teaspoon sugar
salt and pepper
chopped parsley to garnish

Place the aubergine slices on a plate and sprinkle with the salt. Leave for 1 hour then rinse and drain.

Divide the chicken into 8 pieces and remove the skin. Place in a 1.75 litre (3 pint) casserole and cook, uncovered, in a preheated moderately hot oven, 190°C (375°F), Gas Mark 5, for 30 minutes.

Place the aubergine slices in a pan with the remaining ingredients, seasoning to taste with salt and pepper. Bring to the boil, cover and simmer for 10 minutes. Pour into the casserole and return to the oven for 40 to 50 minutes. Serve garnished with chopped parsley.
Serves 4

TURKEY SICILIAN STYLE

25 g (1 oz) butter
1 onion, sliced
75 g (3 oz) button mushrooms, sliced
25 g (1 oz) plain flour
½ teaspoon ground ginger
½ teaspoon grated nutmeg
150 ml (¼ pint) chicken stock
150 ml (¼ pint) skimmed milk
375 g (12 oz) cooked turkey meat, chopped
salt and pepper
15 g (½ oz) flaked almonds, toasted

Melt the butter in a large pan, add the onion and mushrooms and fry for 5 minutes or until soft. Add the flour, ginger and nutmeg. Cook for 1 minute. Gradually blend in the stock and milk. Bring to the boil, stirring, then add the turkey and salt and pepper to taste. Cover and simmer for 20 minutes.

Pile the mixture into a hot serving dish and sprinkle with the toasted almonds. Serve with tagliatelli verdi.
Serves 4

CHICKEN BREASTS WITH CLAM SAUCE

1 tablespoon olive oil
1 tablespoon butter
4 chicken breasts
300 ml (½ pint) clam and tomato juice
3-4 shakes Tabasco
150 ml (¼ pint) water
2 bay leaves
12-16 green olives
salt and pepper
parsley sprigs to garnish

Heat the oil and butter in a large pan, add the chicken breasts and lightly brown. Add the remaining ingredients, except salt and pepper, and simmer, uncovered, for 30 minutes or until the chicken is very tender and the sauce has reduced slightly. Season with salt and pepper to taste, remembering to allow for the saltiness of the olives.

Garnish with parsley and serve with crisply cooked green beans.
Serves 4

ABOVE: *Turkey Sicilian Style*

RIGHT: *Venetian Roast Duck; Braised Wood Pigeons*

VENETIAN ROAST DUCK

1 × 2.25 kg (5 lb)
  duck
salt and pepper
2 teaspoons chopped
  sage
2 celery sticks,
  chopped
1 small onion,
  chopped
1 clove garlic,
  chopped
4 tablespoons
  Marsala
juice of 1 orange
150 ml (¼ pint)
  chicken stock
1 teaspoon lemon
  juice
TO GARNISH:
orange slices
parsley sprigs

Season the duck cavity liberally with salt and pepper and insert the sage, celery, onion and garlic. Prick the skin all over and place the duck breast down on a rack in a roasting tin.

Cook in a preheated moderate oven, 180°C (350°F), Gas Mark 4, for 1½ hours. Drain off the fat from the pan and turn the duck over. Heat the Marsala and orange juice and pour over the duck.

Continue roasting for 1 hour, or until tender, basting occasionally.

Transfer the duck to a warmed serving dish and keep hot. Skim the fat from the pan juices, add the stock and lemon juice and bring to the boil. Check the seasoning and strain into a sauceboat.

Garnish the duck with orange slices and parsley to serve.
Serves 4

BRAISED WOOD PIGEONS

4 wood pigeons
salt and pepper
2 tablespoons oil
25 g (1 oz) butter
1 onion, chopped
2 celery sticks,
  chopped
1 carrot, chopped
50 g (2 oz) streaky
  bacon, derinded
  and chopped
1 sprig each thyme,
  rosemary and sage
150 ml (¼ pint) dry
  white wine
300 ml (½ pint) hot
  chicken stock
375 (12 oz) shelled
  peas

Season the pigeons inside and out with salt and pepper. Heat the oil and butter in a large flameproof casserole, add the onion, celery, carrot, bacon, and herbs tied together, and fry gently for 5 minutes. Add the pigeons and fry, turning until lightly browned.

Add the wine, bring to the boil and boil briskly for about 5 minutes. Add the stock, cover and cook gently for 1 to 1½ hours until the pigeons are almost tender.

Add the peas and cook for 15 to 20 minutes, until the pigeons and peas are tender. Discard the herbs, check the seasoning and serve immediately.
Serves 4

CHICKEN WITH FENNEL

1 × 1.5 kg (3½ lb)
   oven-ready chicken
salt and pepper
175 g (6 oz) cooked
   ham, cut into thick
   strips
2 tablespoons
   chopped fennel
   stalks and leaves
2 cloves garlic,
   crushed
40 g (1½ oz) butter,
   softened
lemon juice
TO GARNISH:
Tuscan Baked
   Fennel (see box tip
   page 67)
fennel leaves

Season the chicken inside and out with salt and pepper. Mix together the ham, fennel and garlic and use to stuff the chicken. Place in a deep casserole dish and spread with the butter.

Cover and cook in a preheated moderately hot oven, 200°C (400°F), Gas Mark 6, for 1 hour. Uncover and continue cooking, basting frequently, for 20 minutes until tender and golden brown. Transfer to a warmed serving dish and keep hot.

Season the juices with salt, pepper and lemon juice to taste and reheat. Garnish the chicken with Tuscan Baked Fennel and fennel leaves. Hand the sauce separately.

Serves 4

MEDITERRANEAN CHICKEN

1.5 kg (3½ lb)
   chicken, halved
50 g (2 oz) butter
4 tablespoons olive
   oil
salt and pepper
2 tablespoons capers
1 tablespoon dried
   thyme
1 lemon, halved

Place the chicken halves in a roasting tin, skin sides up. Prick the skin with a fork or pierce with a sharp knife. Dot with the butter then sprinkle with the oil, salt and pepper to taste, capers and thyme. Squeeze over a little of the juice from the lemons then add the lemon halves to the tin.

Bake in a preheated moderately hot oven, 200°C (400°F), Gas Mark 6, for about 1 hour, until crisp and golden. Serve hot with a crisp green salad.

Serves 4

TURKEY WITH TUNA SAUCE

1 × 4.5 kg (10 lb) oven-ready turkey
1 onion, sliced
1 carrot, sliced
1 bouquet garni
salt and pepper
SAUCE:
1 × 198 g (7 oz) can tuna fish, drained
1 × 50 g (2 oz) can anchovy fillets, drained
1 × 100 g (3½ oz) jar capers
3 tablespoons lemon juice
1 × 500 ml (18 fl oz) jar mayonnaise

Place the turkey in a roasting tin. Pour in 300 ml (½ pint) water and add the onion, carrot, bouquet garni, and salt and pepper to taste. Cover the tin completely with foil and cook in a preheated moderate oven, 160°C (325°F), Gas Mark 3, for 3¾ hours. Leave in the juices in the pan overnight to cool; reserve the juices next day.

Place the tuna fish, anchovies, half the jar of capers with juice, and the lemon juice in a blender or food processor and blend until smooth. Add the mayonnaise and blend until well combined. If the sauce is too thick, mix in a little of the turkey stock.

Carve the turkey, arrange on a large serving platter and coat with the sauce. Use the remaining capers to garnish the turkey.
Serves 20

PRAWN AND CHICKEN PILAFF

2 tablespoons oil
1 small onion, sliced
1-2 cloves garlic, crushed
1 teaspoon ground coriander
250 g (8 oz) chicken breast, diced
500 g (1 lb) cooked long-grain rice
2 large tomatoes, chopped
1 teaspoon basil
175 g (6 oz) peeled prawns
50 g (2 oz) raisins
50 g (2 oz) pine kernels
salt and pepper

Heat the oil in a large frying pan, add the onion and garlic and cook gently for 5 minutes. Add the coriander and chicken and cook for a further 6-8 minutes, stirring constantly.

Stir in the rice, tomatoes and basil, mixing well. Add the prawns, raisins and pine kernels and stir well to mix. Season to taste with salt and pepper and heat through gently for 5 minutes.

Spoon into a warmed serving dish. Serve with a mixed salad.
Serves 4

DUCKLING POMODORO

2.25 kg (5 lb) duckling
25 g (1 oz) butter
1 tablespoon olive oil
½ onion, chopped
1 stick celery, chopped
2 teaspoons plain flour
2 teaspoons tomato purée
397 g (14 oz) can chopped tomatoes
1 teaspoon dried mixed herbs
150 ml (¼ pint) sherry
1 teaspoon sugar
salt and pepper
500 g (1 lb) dried tagliatelle
175 g (6 oz) mushrooms, chopped
4 tablespoons cream

Place the duckling in a large pan, cover with water and poach until tender, about 1½ hours. Drain and cool. Remove and discard the skin and chop the flesh into small pieces.

Melt the butter and oil in a pan, add the onion and celery and cook for 5 minutes. Add the flour and cook for a further 2 minutes. Stir in the tomato purée, tomatoes, herbs, sherry and sugar. Simmer for 10 minutes than add the diced duck and salt and pepper.

Meanwhile, cook the pasta according to the packet instructions until just tender. Drain and place in a heated serving dish. Just before the pasta is cooked, add the chopped mushrooms to the sauce and cook for 3 minutes. Stir in the cream, blending well. Spoon over the cooked pasta.
Serves 6

TUSCAN BAKED FENNEL

The Italians adore fennel and have countless ways of cooking it to serve with meat, poultry and fish alike. In Tuscany the following recipe is popular and is delicious served with poultry: Trim 625 g (1¼ lb) fennel bulbs and remove any discoloured skin with a potato peeler. Cut vertically into 2 cm (¾ inch) thick pieces. Place in a pan with a pinch of salt, 1 thick slice of lemon, 1 tablespoon olive oil and enough boiling water to cover. Cook for 20 minutes then drain well. Melt 25 g (1 oz) butter in a gratin dish, add the fennel and turn to coat. Season to taste with pepper and sprinkle with 25 g (1 oz) Parmesan cheese. Place under a preheated grill until lightly browned. Serve immediately. Serves 4.

LEFT: *Chicken with Fennel*

PHEASANT IN CREAM SAUCE

1 pheasant
salt and pepper
1 small onion, peeled
1 tablespoon oil
25 g (1 oz) butter
142 ml (¼ pint)
    carton double
    cream
2 teaspoons lemon
    juice
TO GARNISH:
cooked peas
cooked small carrots

Season the cavity of the pheasant liberally with salt and pepper and insert the onion. Heat the oil and butter in a flameproof casserole, add the pheasant and brown lightly all over.

Turn the bird breast side down. Cover and cook in a preheated moderate oven, 180°C (350°F), Gas Mark 4, for 30 minutes. Turn the pheasant, pour over the cream and continue cooking, basting occasionally, for 20 to 30 minutes until tender.

Transfer the pheasant to a warmed serving dish and keep hot. Add the lemon juice to the sauce and season with salt and pepper to taste. Cook, stirring, over moderate heat until smooth and thickened.

Pour over the pheasant and garnish with peas and carrots to serve.
Serves 4

RABBIT STEWED WITH VEGETABLES

1 aubergine, cut into
    2.5 cm (1 inch)
    cubes
salt and pepper
3 tablespoons oil
2 rashers streaky
    bacon, derinded
    and diced
1 celery stick,
    chopped
1 kg (2 lb) rabbit
    portions
4 large tomatoes,
    skinned and
    chopped
1 clove garlic,
    chopped
2 teaspoons each
    chopped marjoram
    and parsley
4 tablespoons
    Marsala
200 ml (7 fl oz)
    chicken stock
1 red or green pepper,
    cored, deseeded and
    thinly sliced

Place the aubergine in a colander, sprinkle with salt and leave for 1 hour. Drain, rinse and dry on kitchen paper.

Meanwhile, heat the oil in a large pan, add the bacon and celery and fry gently for 2 minutes. Add the rabbit portions and fry until lightly browned. Add the tomatoes, garlic, herbs and a little salt and pepper and cook, stirring, for 1 to 2 minutes.

Add the Marsala, bring to the boil and simmer for about 5 minutes until well reduced. Add the stock, cover and simmer for 30 minutes.

Add the aubergine and pepper and simmer for 30 minutes or until the rabbit is tender. Transfer the rabbit to a warmed serving dish and keep hot.

If the sauce is too thin, boil briskly for about 5 minutes until well reduced. Check the seasoning and spoon over the rabbit.
Serves 4

NOTE: Chicken portions could be used instead of rabbit.

| GAME CHIPS |

There are many accompaniments to poultry and game in Italy but game chips are most popular. To make enough to serve 3 to 4 people, soak 500 g (1 lb) thinly sliced potatoes in salted water for 1 hour. Drain, dry very thoroughly and deep-fry small quantities at a time in hot oil for 2 to 3 minutes until light golden. Drain on kitchen paper. Just before serving deep-fry again for 2 to 3 minutes until very crisp. Drain and sprinkle with salt to serve.

LEFT: *Rabbit Stewed with Vegetables*

RIGHT: *Chicken with Peppers; Chicken in Egg and Lemon Sauce*

CHICKEN WITH PEPPERS

flour for coating
salt and pepper
4 chicken portions
3 tablespoons oil
1 onion, thinly sliced
1 clove garlic, crushed
4 tablespoons dry
 white Vermouth
1 teaspoon chopped
 marjoram
1 × 227 g (8 oz) can
 tomatoes
1 teaspoon sugar
1 large green pepper,
 cored, deseeded and
 sliced

Season the flour with salt and pepper and use to coat the chicken. Heat the oil in a large pan, add the onion and chicken and fry gently for 10 minutes until golden. Pour off surplus oil.

Add the garlic, Vermouth and marjoram to the pan and simmer until the wine has almost completely evaporated. Add the tomatoes with their juice, the sugar and green pepper. Cover and simmer for 30 minutes or until the chicken is cooked. Lift the chicken onto a warmed serving dish and keep hot.

Boil the sauce briskly, uncovered, until reduced to a coating consistency. Check the seasoning and spoon over the chicken to serve.
Serves 4

CHICKEN IN EGG AND LEMON SAUCE

4 chicken portions
salt and pepper
2 tablespoons oil
25 g (1 oz) butter
25 g (1 oz) plain
 flour
300 ml (1/2 pint)
 chicken stock
1 bay leaf
1 small marjoram
 sprig
2 egg yolks
1 tablespoon lemon
 juice
TO GARNISH:
1 tablespoon chopped
 parsley
lemon slices

Season the chicken with salt and pepper. Heat the oil and butter in a pan, add the chicken and fry gently for about 12 minutes until golden. Remove and set aside. Pour off all but 2 tablespoons of the fat.

Add the flour to the pan and cook, stirring, for 1 minute. Add the stock and bring to the boil, stirring. Return the chicken to the pan and add the bay leaf and marjoram. Cover and simmer for 30 minutes, until tender.

Transfer the chicken to a warmed serving dish. Discard the herbs. Blend the egg yolks and lemon juice with 3 tablespoons of the sauce. Add to the pan and heat gently, stirring, until thickened; do not boil. Adjust seasoning and pour over the chicken. Garnish with parsley and lemon.
Serves 4

CHICKEN WITH PASTA

1 × 1.5 kg (3½ lb) oven-ready chicken with giblets
2 cloves garlic, crushed
3 tablespoons olive oil
1 × 397 g (14 oz) can chopped tomatoes
1 teaspoon dried oregano
450 ml (¾ pint) chicken stock or water
250 g (8 oz) dried conchiglie or tagliatelle
salt and pepper

Remove the giblets and set aside. Truss the chicken securely. Rub the bird all over with the garlic and some of the oil. Place in a roasting tin and surround with the giblets, tomatoes with their juice, oregano and 1 tablespoon of the oil. Cover loosely with foil and cook in a preheated moderate oven, 180°C (350°F), Gas Mark 4, for 1 to 1¼ hours.

Remove the foil and add the stock or water and pasta, stirring well so the pasta is thoroughly moistened. Dribble the remaining oil over all and add salt and pepper to taste. Return to the oven, uncovered, and cook for 45 minutes, until the pasta is cooked and the chicken is very tender.

Serve with okra.
Serves 4

CHICKEN CACCIATORE

6 or 12 chicken pieces
salt and pepper
50 g (2 oz) butter
3 tablespoons olive oil
1 onion, chopped
2 cloves garlic, crushed
125 g (4 oz) button mushrooms, sliced
150 ml (¼ pint) dry white wine
4 tablespoons chicken stock
1 × 227 g (8 oz) can tomatoes, drained and chopped
4 tablespoons tomato purée
2 bay leaves
1 teaspoon dried basil
2 tablespoons brandy

Rub the chicken pieces with salt and pepper. Melt the butter with the oil in a flameproof casserole. Add the chicken pieces, in batches, and brown on all sides; remove from the casserole as they brown.

Add the onion and garlic to the casserole and fry until softened. Add the mushrooms and fry for 2 minutes. Stir in the wine, stock, tomatoes, tomato purée, bay leaves and basil and bring to the boil.

Return the chicken pieces to the casserole and simmer, uncovered, for 10 minutes. Cover and continue simmering for 20 minutes or until the chicken is cooked through. Stir in the brandy, adjust the seasoning and serve.
Serves 6

CHICKEN WITH MUSHROOMS

2 tablespoons olive oil
15 g (½ oz) butter
1.5 kg (3½ lb) chicken, jointed
150 ml (¼ pint) dry white wine
500 g (1 lb) mixed mushrooms
4 tomatoes, skinned and chopped
1 tablespoon chopped parsley
1 teaspoon chopped basil
salt and pepper

Heat the oil and butter in a flameproof casserole, add the chicken pieces and fry until browned on all sides.

Add the wine, mushrooms, tomatoes, parsley, basil and salt and pepper to taste. Bring to the boil, reduce the heat, then simmer for about 25 minutes until the chicken is cooked and tender.

Serve hot with cooked pasta and a crisp seasonal salad.
Serves 4

LEFT: *Chicken with Pasta*

RIGHT: *Creamy Chicken Livers with Port*

ITALIAN CHICKEN

4 chicken breasts,
  skinned and boned
50 g (2 oz) lean
  ham, cut into 4
  pieces
150 ml (¼ pint)
  chicken stock
1 tablespoon sherry
1 red pepper, cored,
  deseeded and sliced
STUFFING:
40 g (1½ oz)
  breadcrumbs
50 g (2 oz) Parmesan
  cheese, grated
1 small onion, finely
  chopped
2 teaspoons chopped
  parsley
1 tablespoon sherry
salt and pepper
TO GARNISH:
watercress sprigs

Mix together the stuffing ingredients, with salt and pepper to taste, and press onto the cut flesh on the underside of the chicken breasts. Place a piece of ham over the top. Arrange the chicken in a casserole, pour over the stock and sherry and add the red pepper.

Cover and cook in a preheated moderate oven, 180°C (350°F), Gas Mark 4, for 1 hour or until the chicken is cooked, basting occasionally with the liquid. Garnish with watercress.

Serves 4

VENETIAN CHICKEN

250 g (8 oz) Ricotta
  cheese
2 tablespoons milk
3 tablespoons
  chopped mixed
  herbs (parsley,
  rosemary, basil,
  sage and
  marjoram)
salt and pepper
1.5 kg (3½ lb)
  oven-ready chicken
15 g (½ oz) butter

Mix the cheese with the milk, herbs and salt and pepper to taste. Working from the neck end of the chicken, carefully loosen away the breast skin from the flesh with your hand to make a large pocket to hold the cheese and herb stuffing. Push the stuffing into the pocket, smoothing and pressing the mixture evenly over the flesh. Close up the opening at the neck end and secure by sewing with a needle and thread.

Place the chicken in a roasting tin, dot with the butter and roast in a preheated hot oven 230°C (450°F), Gas Mark 8, for 10 minutes. Reduce the oven temperature to 180°C (350°F), Gas 4, and cook for a further 1 hour, basting with the cooking juices. Serve hot.

Serves 4

CREAMY CHICKEN LIVERS WITH PORT

25 g (1 oz) butter
1 tablespoon oil
500 g (1 lb) chicken
  livers, trimmed
  and halved
3 celery sticks, sliced
4 tablespoons port
142 ml (¼ pint) carton
  soured cream
salt and pepper
celery leaves to
  garnish

Heat the butter and oil in a pan, add the livers and celery and fry gently for 3 to 4 minutes, until the livers are golden outside but still pink inside. Add the port and simmer for a few minutes, until slightly reduced. Add the soured cream, tilting the pan to mix, and continue cooking gently until a smooth sauce forms. Season with salt and pepper to taste.

Garnish with celery leaves and serve with pasta tossed in a garlic-flavoured butter.

Serves 4

CHICKEN WITH LANGOUSTINES

50 g (2 oz) butter
4 chicken drumsticks
4 chicken thighs
125 g (4 oz) button
  mushrooms
8 large prawns,
  peeled
2 tablespoons
  chopped parsley
SAUCE:
1 tablespoon oil
1 onion, finely
  chopped
2 cloves garlic,
  crushed
397 g (14 oz) can
  chopped tomatoes
  with herbs
1 teaspoon dried
  oregano
1 teaspoon brown
  sugar
salt and pepper
250 ml (8 fl oz) red
  wine

First prepare the sauce by heating the oil in a pan. Add the onion and garlic and cook until softened, about 5 minutes. Add the tomatoes, oregano, sugar, salt and pepper to taste and wine, mixing well. Bring to the boil, reduce the heat and simmer for 15 minutes, until thickened.

Melt the butter in a frying pan, add the chicken and cook until golden on all sides. Add the tomato sauce and mushrooms and simmer, covered, for 30 minutes.

About 5 minutes before the end of the cooking time, add the prawns and cook until tender. Serve hot, garnished with the chopped parsley.
Serves 4

CREAMED CHICKEN WITH NOODLES

2 × 2.25 kg (5 lb)
  oven-ready
  chickens
3 large onions,
  halved
1 bottle dry white
  wine
1 large bouquet garni
salt and pepper
125 g (4 oz) butter
8 shallots, chopped
3-4 cloves garlic,
  crushed
1 kg (2 lb) tomatoes,
  skinned, deseeded
  and chopped
2 tablespoons each
  chopped basil and
  parsley
3 tablespoons
  chopped thyme
2 × 284 ml (½ pint)
  cartons double
  cream
2 kg (4½ lb) fresh
  tagliatelle
125 g (4 oz) butter
fresh herbs to garnish

Place the chickens in a large roasting tin. Add the onions, wine, bouquet garni, and salt and pepper to taste. Cover with foil and cook in a preheated moderate oven, 180°C (350°F), Gas Mark 4, for 2½ hours, until very tender; cool.

Remove the flesh from the chickens and cut into small pieces. Remove the fat from the top of the liquid and strain the stock.

Melt the butter in a large pan, add the shallots and garlic and cook gently for 10 minutes. Add the tomatoes and herbs, and season with salt and pepper. Stir in the strained stock.

Bring to the boil, cover and simmer for 40 minutes. Remove lid and cook rapidly until thickened. Stir in the cream and chicken; set aside.

Cook the tagliatelle in 2 large pans until al dente. Drain and return to the pans. Divide the butter between the pans and toss well.

Heat the sauce, without boiling, pour over the pasta and toss well.

Transfer to a warmed serving dish and garnish with herbs. Serve with grated Parmesan cheese.
Serves 20

Creamed Chicken with Noodles

ITALIAN BRAISED CHICKEN

3 tablespoons olive
  oil
1 small onion, sliced
2 cloves garlic,
  crushed
1.25 kg (3 lb)
  chicken, cut into
  small pieces
1 small piece canned
  pimiento, chopped
salt and pepper
1 tablespoon tomato
  purée
3-5 tablespoons dry
  white wine
1 sprig fresh
  rosemary, chopped
6-8 tablespoons
  chicken stock
fresh rosemary sprigs,
  to garnish

Heat the oil in a flameproof casserole, add the onion and garlic and fry gently for 15 minutes. Add the chicken pieces with the pimiento and salt and pepper to taste and fry over a moderate heat, turning occasionally, until browned on all sides.

Mix the tomato purée with the wine and stir into the chicken mixture. Reduce the heat, cover and simmer gently for 30 minutes.

Add the chopped rosemary and cook for a further 30 minutes or until the chicken is tender, adding a little stock occasionally to moisten. Serve hot, garnished with rosemary sprigs.
Serves 4

Italian Braised Chicken

ROMAN PEPPERED CHICKEN

4 tablespoons olive
  oil
2 cloves garlic, finely
  chopped
1 onion, chopped
1.5 kg (3½ lb) chicken,
  cut into pieces
2 red peppers, cored,
  deseeded and sliced
1 yellow pepper,
  cored, deseeded and
  sliced
2 teaspoons chopped
  marjoram and basil
salt and pepper

Heat the oil in a flameproof casserole, add the garlic, onion and chicken and fry until browned on all sides.

Add the peppers, marjoram, basil and salt and pepper to taste. Cover and cook gently, stirring occasionally and adding a little water to moisten if the mixture appears to be too dry, for about 25 minutes until the chicken is cooked and tender.

Serve hot with pasta or rice and a crisp seasonal salad.
Serves 4

GRILLED LEMON CHICKEN

1.5 kg (3½ lb)
  chicken
5 tablespoons olive
  oil
3 tablespoons lemon
  juice
2 teaspoons chopped
  rosemary
salt and pepper
1 tablespoon chopped
  parsley
lemon slices to
  garnish

Halve the chicken along the breast bone and open out flat, hold in place with a long skewer. Cut the wing and leg joints just enough to spread them flat so that they do not cook too quickly or burn during grilling.

Place the chicken in a dish. Mix the oil with the lemon juice, rosemary and salt and pepper to taste. Pour over the chicken and leave to marinate for 1 hour.

To cook, remove the chicken from the marinade and place under a preheated low to moderate grill. Cook for about 30 to 40 minutes, turning over frequently and basting with the marinade during cooking. The chicken is cooked when the thigh juices run clear.

Serve hot sprinkled with the parsley and garnished with the lemon slices.
Serves 4

PASTA AND RICE

Pasta and rice reflect the somewhat hazy but real culinary divide between the north and south of Italy. Rice is popular with the inhabitants of northern Italy where risotto is cooked and served in perhaps almost as many different ways as pasta; and pasta is the prime favourite with those in the south.

The famous Italian dish of risotto is made using risotto rice and is cooked in a special way like no other rice dish. The rice is cooked carefully on top of the stove with the addition of gradual amounts of stock until it has a creamy consistency but the rice grains still remain firm with a slight bite. Meat, fish, vegetables and cheeses are often added to the dish during cooking.

Pasta is also cooked to perfection on top of the stove, but this time with copious amounts of water. The Italians say it should be cooked *al dente*. This means it is cooked until just tender and still has a slight bite to it. The pasta may be plain, enriched with egg, made with wholemeal flour or flavoured with spinach or tomato purée. The shapes and sizes available are immense, ranging from the tiny alphabet and soup pasta to the large cannelloni and shell pasta.

Whether you choose pasta or rice you can be sure that you are choosing an excellent food to include in a healthy diet since all are low in fat and reasonably low in calories.

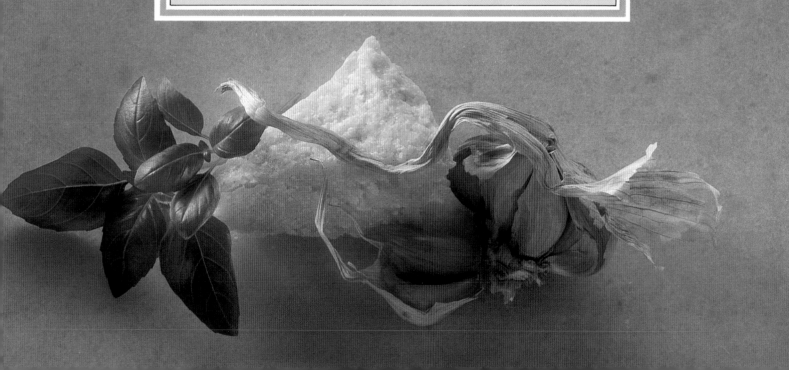

SPAGHETTI BOLOGNAISE

BOLOGNAISE SAUCE:
25 g (1 oz) butter
2 tablespoons oil
2 onions, chopped
500 g (1 lb) minced
   beef
125 g (4 oz)
   mushrooms,
   chopped
1 × 397 g (14 oz)
   can chopped
   tomatoes
2 cloves garlic,
   crushed
1/2 teaspoon dried
   oregano
4 tablespoons tomato
   purée
150 ml (1/4 pint) beef
   stock or red wine
salt and pepper
SPAGHETTI:
250-375 (8-12 oz)
   dried spaghetti
25 g (1 oz) butter
grated nutmeg
TO GARNISH:
grated Parmesan
   cheese

To make the Bolognaise sauce: Heat the butter and oil in a saucepan, add the onion and fry until softened. Add the meat and fry briskly, stirring, until evenly browned. Drain off all the excess fat, then add the remaining sauce ingredients, with salt and pepper to taste.

Bring to simmering point, stirring, then cover and simmer over low heat for 1 hour, adding more liquid if necessary.

Cook the spaghetti in boiling salted water according to packet instructions and drain thoroughly. Melt the butter in the saucepan, return the spaghetti to the pan and toss well. Season to taste with nutmeg and pepper.

Turn into a serving dish, top with the Bolognaise sauce and sprinkle with Parmesan cheese.
Serves 4

SAVOURY BAKED MACARONI

2 tablespoons oil
1 large onion, finely
   chopped
2 cloves garlic,
   crushed
1 small chilli,
   deseeded and finely
   chopped
4 rashers smoked
   streaky bacon,
   derinded and
   chopped
1 × 400 g (14 oz)
   can peeled
   tomatoes
1 teaspoon sugar
salt
250 g (8 oz) dried
   short-cut macaroni
50 g (2 oz) grated
   Provolone or other
   hard cheese

Heat the oil in a saucepan, add the onion, garlic, chilli and bacon and fry gently for 10 minutes, stirring occasionally. Add the tomatoes with their juice, the sugar, and salt to taste. Bring to the boil, stirring, cover and simmer for 20 minutes.

Cook the macaroni in boiling salted water according to the packet instructions; drain thoroughly.

Arrange alternate layers of pasta, sauce and cheese in an oiled ovenproof dish, finishing with cheese.

Serve immediately, or cover and leave in a preheated cool oven, 140°C (275°F), Gas Mark 1, for 20 to 30 minutes to allow the flavours to blend.
Serves 3 to 4

TAGLIARINI WITH TUNA

1 × 198 g (7 oz) can
   tuna fish, in oil
1 clove garlic, crushed
2 tablespoons
   chopped parsley
250 g (8 oz) ripe
   tomatoes, skinned
   and chopped
150 ml (1/4 pint)
   chicken stock
salt and pepper
375 g (12 oz) dried
   tagliarini

Drain the oil from the tuna into a pan, add the garlic and heat gently for 2 minutes. Add the parsley and tomatoes and cook until the tomatoes begin to soften. Flake the tuna and add to the pan with the stock, and salt and pepper to taste. Simmer while cooking the pasta.

Cook the pasta in boiling salted water until al dente; drain well. Turn into a warmed serving dish. Add the sauce, toss and serve immediately.
Serves 4

SPAGHETTI CARBONARA

375 g (12 oz) dried
  spaghetti
salt and pepper
175 g (6 oz) streaky
  bacon, derinded
  and chopped
3 eggs
3 tablespoons cream
40 g (1½ oz) grated
  Parmesan cheese
40 g (1½ oz) butter

Cook the pasta in boiling salted water according to the packet instructions; drain.

Meanwhile, fry the bacon in its own fat until crisp. Drain well.

Beat the eggs with the cream, cheese, a little salt and plenty of pepper. Melt the butter in a large saucepan, add the egg mixture and stir until just beginning to thicken. Add the spaghetti and bacon, mix well and serve immediately.
Serves 4

FETTUCCINE WITH GORGONZOLA

375 g (12 oz) dried
  fettuccine
salt and pepper
25 g (1 oz) butter
5 tablespoons milk
125 g (4 oz)
  Gorgonzola
  cheese, diced
125 ml (4 fl oz)
  double cream
25 g (1 oz) grated
  Parmesan cheese
1-2 tablespoons
  chopped basil
  (optional)

Cook the pasta in boiling salted water according to the packet instructions. Drain thoroughly.

Meanwhile, put the butter, milk and Gorgonzola cheese into a flameproof casserole. Place over a moderate heat and mash the cheese to a creamy sauce. Add the cream, and salt and pepper to taste and heat to simmering point.

Stir in the pasta, Parmesan cheese and basil if using. Toss until the pasta is coated, then serve immediately with extra Parmesan cheese.
Serves 4

LEFT: *Savoury Baked Macaroni*

RIGHT: *Tagliarini with Tuna; Spaghetti Carbonara; Fettuccine with Gorgonzola*

CANNELLONI FLORENTINE

12 tubes cannelloni
1 cucumber
250 g (8 oz) button
  mushrooms,
  quartered
FILLING:
125 g (4 oz) ham,
  diced
250 g (8 oz) frozen
  chopped spinach,
  thawed
2 tablespoons grated
  Parmesan cheese
grated nutmeg
salt and pepper
SAUCE:
2 cloves garlic,
  crushed
1 × 540 ml (19 fl
  oz) can tomato
  juice
1 bay leaf
1 tablespoon lemon
  juice
few dashes of
  Worcestershire and
  Tabasco sauces
TOPPING:
5 slices processed
  Cheddar cheese

Mix the filling ingredients together, seasoning with nutmeg, salt and pepper to taste, and use to fill the cannelloni.

Mix together the sauce ingredients, adding salt and pepper to taste. Pour a little sauce into an ovenproof dish large enough to take the cannelloni in a single layer. Place the cannelloni on top and pour over the remaining sauce. Cut the cucumber into 1 cm (½ inch) slices, then into quarters. Arrange along each side of the cannelloni with the mushrooms.

Cover with foil and bake in a preheated hot oven, 220°C (425°F), Gas Mark 7, for 30 minutes. Remove the bay leaf.

Cut the cheese into thin strips, sprinkle on top of the cannelloni and return to the oven for 10 minutes, until golden.

Serve with a green salad.

Serves 4

SPAGHETTI WITH MUSSEL AND TOMATO SAUCE

1 kg (2 lb) fresh
  mussels in shells
3 tablespoons olive
  oil
1 onion, chopped
1 clove garlic, crushed
500 g (1 lb)
  tomatoes, skinned
  and chopped, or
  400 g (14 oz) can
  chopped tomatoes
2 teaspoons tomato
  purée
3 tablespoons dry
  white wine
375 g (12 oz) dried
  spaghetti
salt and pepper
1 tablespoon chopped
  parsley

Discard any opened mussels. Scrub the remainder and wash them thoroughly in cold water. Place them in a large pan, cover and cook over high heat for 4 minutes, stirring once or twice.

Lift out the mussels, discard any unopened ones, and remove the others from their shells.

Drain the liquid into a small pan through a sieve lined with muslin and boil to reduce to 2 tablespoons.

Heat the oil in a pan and fry the onion and garlic for 4 to 5 minutes. Add the tomatoes, tomato purée, mussel liquid and wine and cook until it thickens. Add the mussels, season to taste and heat gently.

Cook the spaghetti in a large pan of boiling, salted water until al dente. Drain. Transfer to a warmed dish, pour on the sauce and sprinkle with parsley.

Serves 4

PARMESAN CHEESE

Genuine Parmesan cheese is made under strictly controlled conditions in restricted areas of Italy; imitations are poor substitutes for the real thing. Its exquisite flavour and granular texture have made it a world-famous grating cheese for pasta, but in Italy it is also enjoyed as a table cheese when young. A genuine cheese is a large golden drum with the words Parmigiano Reggiano pricked all over the bulging sides. It must be matured for at least 1 year; more expensive grades are matured for up to 4 years and develop an even finer flavour.

MACARONI WITH PRAWN AND MUSSEL SAUCE

75 ml (3 fl oz) olive oil
1 large onion, finely chopped
2 cloves garlic, crushed
800 g (1 lb 12 oz) can tomatoes, chopped
150 ml (¼ pint) dry white wine
pinch of brown sugar
½ teaspoon dried thyme
salt and pepper
500 g (1 lb) peeled prawns
125 g (4 oz) cooked or canned shelled mussels
400 g (13 oz) dried macaroni
chopped parsley, to garnish

Heat the oil in a large heavy-based pan. Add the onion and garlic and cook until golden. Add the tomatoes and their juice, wine, sugar, thyme and salt and pepper to taste. Bring to the boil, reduce the heat and simmer gently for 15-20 minutes.

Stir in the prawns and mussels and cook for a further 3 minutes, stirring occasionally.

Meanwhile, cook the macaroni in boiling salted water, according to the packet instructions, until just tender.

Drain the pasta and arrange on a warmed serving dish. Spoon the sauce over and sprinkle with chopped parsley to serve.

Serves 4 to 6

FETTUCCINE IN FOUR CHEESES

500 g (1 lb) dried fettuccine
good pinch of salt
2 tablespoons oil
1 onion
2 cloves garlic
SAUCE:
25 g (1 oz) butter
2 cloves garlic, sliced
50 g (2 oz) each Emmental, Mozzarella, Parmesan and Cheddar, grated
175 ml (6 fl oz) single cream
salt and pepper
TO GARNISH:
1 tablespoon each chopped parsley and basil

Place the pasta, salt, oil, onion and garlic in a large pan of boiling water and cook for 8 to 9 minutes, until the pasta is just cooked.

Meanwhile, make the sauce. Melt the butter in a pan, add the garlic and cook, without browning, for 3 minutes. Stir in the cheeses and cream and continue stirring over a low heat until the cheeses have melted. Season with salt and pepper to taste.

Drain the pasta and remove the onion and garlic. Toss the pasta in the sauce, sprinkle with the herbs and serve immediately, with a tomato and onion salad.

Serves 4

QUICK PASTA SAUCES

Pasta and sauces are culinary partners and chosen carefully, even when time is at a premium, can bring rich rewards. There are three basic sauces for pasta – a cream sauce, tomato sauce or green sauce. The additions you make to these basics can be truly inspiring. To each and every one you could add any of the following to make a memorable pasta sauce: mussels cooked in wine; salami or smoked ham strips; diced and fried crisp bacon; finely chopped olives or capers; chopped or sliced mushrooms; finely chopped fresh herbs; skinned, deseeded and chopped fresh tomatoes; cooked and quartered artichoke hearts; coarsely chopped or sliced Parma ham or peperoni; coarsely chopped and blanched spinach; freshly cooked prawns and other seafood; lightly steamed tiny broccoli florets; grated fresh Parmesan cheese; and crumbled or chopped pine kernels and walnuts.

RIGHT: *Fettuccine in Four Cheeses*

HAM AND MUSHROOM LASAGNE

4 tablespoons oil
75 g (3 oz) butter
1 small onion, chopped
300 ml (½ pint) dry white wine
3 large tomatoes, skinned, deseeded and chopped
750 g (1½ lb) button mushrooms, sliced
1-2 cloves garlic, crushed
1 teaspoon dried mixed herbs
2 tablespoons chopped parsley
salt and pepper
300 g (10 oz) no precook lasagne
450 ml (¾ pint) Béchamel Sauce (see page 153)
375 g (12 oz)
375 g (12 oz) unsmoked ham, cut into thin strips
1 × 400 g (14 oz) can artichoke hearts, drained and sliced
50 g (2 oz) Parmesan cheese, grated

Heat the oil and butter in a pan, add the onion and cook for 2 minutes. Add the wine and tomatoes, bring to the boil and simmer for 20 minutes, stirring occasionally, until the liquid has evaporated.

Stir in the mushrooms, garlic and mixed herbs and cook for 6 to 7 minutes, until thickened. Add the parsley, and salt and pepper to taste.

Line the base of a large buttered ovenproof dish with lasagne. Spoon over some mushrooms, then a little Béchamel sauce. Sprinkle with ham and artichoke. Repeat the layers, finishing with pasta and Béchamel sauce.

Sprinkle with the Parmesan and bake in a preheated moderately hot oven, 200°C (400°F), Gas Mark 6 for 20 to 25 minutes until golden brown. Serve immediately.
Serves 6

MUSHROOM AND PRAWN RISOTTO

4 dried cêpes, or 50 g (2 oz) flat open mushrooms
2 cloves garlic
1 large onion
1 tablespoon oil
15 g (½ oz) butter
175 g (6 oz) Italian risotto rice
grated rind of 1 lemon
1 tablespoon capers
2 tablespoons chopped parsley
salt and pepper
300 ml (½ pint) dry white wine
300 ml (½ pint) fish or chicken stock
1 tablespoon tomato purée
250 g (8 oz) peeled prawns
4 cooked whole prawns to garnish

Soak the cêpes, if using, in warm water for 15 minutes; squeeze dry. Slice the cêpes or mushrooms.

Slice the garlic thinly and chop the onion finely. Heat the oil and butter in a pan, add the garlic and onion and fry gently until browned. Add the cêpes or mushrooms, stir in the rice and cook for 1 minute.

Add the lemon rind, capers, parsley and salt and pepper to taste; mix well. Pour over the wine and stock. Bring to the boil and cook, uncovered, for 12 to 15 minutes until the rice is firm.

Stir in the tomato purée and increase the heat to reduce any excess liquid. Stir in the prawns. Garnish with whole prawns and serve immediately.
Serves 4

ABOVE: *Ham and Mushroom Lasagne*

RIGHT: *Lasagne with Ricotta Pesto; Spaghetti with Bacon Sauce*

LASAGNE WITH RICOTTA PESTO

200 g (7 oz) basil leaves
175 ml (6 fl oz) olive oil
75 g (3 oz) pine kernels
4 cloves garlic, chopped
175 g (6oz) Parmesan, grated
25 g (1 oz) Cheddar cheese, grated
50 g (2 oz) Ricotta or curd cheese
salt
50 g (2 oz) butter, softened
250 g (8 oz) quantity pasta dough (see page 150)
basil sprigs to garnish

Put the basil, oil, pine kernels and garlic in an electric blender or food processor and work until smooth. Transfer to a bowl and stir in the cheeses and salt to taste. Beat in the butter.

Cut the pasta into 8 × 13 cm (3 × 5 inch) lengths and cook, in two batches, for about 1 minute, until *al dente*. Drain and keep warm.

Add 1 tablespoon of the cooking water to the pesto and mix well.

Arrange a quarter of the lasagne on a warmed serving dish and cover with a quarter of the pesto. Repeat the layers. Garnish with basil and serve immediately.

Serves 4 to 6

SPAGHETTI WITH BACON SAUCE

500 g (1 lb) fresh spaghetti
125 g (4 oz) bacon, chopped
50 g (2 oz) butter
2 cloves garlic, crushed
3 eggs
142 ml (¼ pint) carton double cream
75g (3 oz) Cheddar cheese, grated
50 g (2 oz) Parmesan cheese, grated
1 teaspoon mustard
salt and pepper
thyme to garnish

Cook the spaghetti until *al dente*. Meanwhile fry the bacon in its own fat until crisp. Drain the pasta thoroughly, return to the pan, add the butter and toss well. Stir in the garlic and bacon.

Beat together the eggs, cream, cheeses and mustard. Season with a little salt and plenty of pepper and add the herbs.

Pour the mixture over the spaghetti and stir over a gentle heat until the sauce is creamy, taking care not to 'scramble' the eggs. Transfer to a warmed serving dish and garnish with thyme. Serve immediately, accompanied by Parmesan cheese.

Serves 4 to 6

SEAFOOD CANNELLONI

2 celery sticks,
    chopped
2 carrots, chopped
600 ml (1 pint) milk
1 onion, quartered
3 peppercorns
1 bay leaf
50 g (2 oz) butter
50 g (2 oz) flour
1 tablespoon chopped
    dill
2 tablespoons snipped
    chives
salt and pepper
250 g (8 oz) quantity
    pasta dough (see
    page 150)
1 tablespoon oil
2 tablespoons dried
    breadcrumbs
FILLING:
15 g (½ oz) butter
2 spring onions,
    chopped
50 g (2 oz) button
    mushrooms, finely
    chopped
150 ml (¼ pint) dry
    white wine
125 g (4 oz) peeled
    prawns
125 g (4 oz) cooked
    or canned crab
    meat, flaked
125 g (4 oz)
    Cheddar cheese,
    grated
4 tablespoons grated
    Parmesan cheese
prawns and dill
    sprigs, to garnish

Put the celery and carrots in a pan with the milk, onion, peppercorns and bay leaf. Bring to the boil, remove from the heat and leave until cold. Strain and reserve the milk.

Melt the butter in a pan, add the flour and cook for 2 minutes, stirring constantly. Gradually add the milk, bring to the boil and cook for 2 minutes, stirring constantly, until smooth, boiling and thickened. Stir in the dill and chives with salt and pepper to taste.

To make the filling, melt the butter in a pan, add the spring onions and mushrooms and cook for 1 minute. Add the wine and boil to reduce the wine to about 1 to 2 tablespoons. Remove from the heat, stir in just over one quarter of the sauce and mix well. Add the prawns, crab meat and salt and pepper to taste. Stir in the cheeses, heating if necessary to melt.

Roll out the pasta dough thinly. Cut into 8 × 10 cm (3 × 4 inch) sheets and cook in boiling salted water, with the oil added, for 1 minute. Drain thoroughly and lay on clean tea towels.

Divide the seafood filling between the pasta sheets and roll up from the shorter side. Arrange in a single layer, seam side down, in a lightly greased ovenproof dish. Spoon over the remaining sauce and sprinkle with the breadcrumbs.

Cook in a preheated moderately hot oven, 200°C (400°F), Gas Mark 6, for 15 to 20 minutes, until golden. Garnish with prawns and dill sprigs and serve at once.
Serves 4

NOODLES WITH PESTO

4 cloves garlic
about 35 basil leaves
about 25 marjoram
    leaves
50 g (2 oz) butter
284 ml (½ pint)
    carton double
    cream
salt and pepper
500 g (1 lb) fresh
    tagliatelle
150 g (5 oz)
    Parmesan cheese,
    grated
basil or marjoram
    sprigs to garnish

Crush the garlic and finely chop the herbs. Mix together well. Melt half the butter in a pan, remove from the heat, stir in the cream, and season well with salt and pepper.

Cook the pasta until al dente. Drain well and turn into a warmed serving dish. Add the remaining butter and toss well.

Return the sauce to the heat and stir in the cheese until melted. Pour over the pasta and toss well. Garnish with basil or marjoram and serve immediately.
Serves 6

SAVOURY MACARONI CHEESE

500 g (1 lb) dried
    short-cut macaroni
salt
4 rashers bacon,
    derinded and
    chopped
2 onions, chopped
2 × 300 ml (½ pint)
    packets cheese
    sauce mix
600 ml (1 pint) milk
125 ml (4 fl oz)
    single cream
175 g (6 oz)
    Cheddar cheese,
    grated
1 × 400 g (14 oz)
    can tomatoes,
    drained and
    chopped
TO GARNISH:
tomato slices
parsley sprigs

Cook the macaroni in plenty of boiling salted water according to the packet instructions.

Cook the bacon in a frying pan over low heat until the fat runs. Add the onions and fry gently for 5 minutes.

Make up the cheese sauce with the milk as directed on the packet, then add to the bacon and onions. Stir in the cream and half the cheese. Cook gently until the cheese is melted.

Drain the macaroni and add to the sauce, with the tomatoes; mix well.

Turn into a shallow flameproof dish and top with the remaining cheese. Place under a preheated hot grill for 10 minutes or until the top is crisp and brown. Garnish with tomato and parsley. Serve immediately.
Serves 4

Seafood Cannelloni; Noodles with Pesto

SPINACH CANNELLONI

500 g (1 lb) frozen
   chopped spinach,
   thawed
175 g (6 oz) matured
   Cheddar cheese,
   grated
50 g (2 oz) fresh
   breadcrumbs
salt and pepper
grated nutmeg
8 tubes cannelloni
25 g (1 oz) butter
25 g (1 oz) plain
   flour
300 ml (½ pint)
   milk
1 teaspoon mild
   French mustard

Drain the spinach thoroughly and mix with 50 g (2 oz) of the cheese, 40 g (1½ oz) of the breadcrumbs, and salt, pepper and nutmeg to taste.

Divide the spinach mixture between the cannelloni. Place in a greased shallow ovenproof dish.

Melt the butter in a pan, stir in the flour and cook for 1 minute. Slowly blend in the milk, then heat, stirring, until the sauce thickens. Add 75 g (3 oz) of the cheese, the mustard, and salt and pepper to taste. Pour over the cannelloni. Mix the remaining breadcrumbs and cheese, and sprinkle over the sauce.

Bake in a moderately hot oven, 200°C (400°F), Gas Mark 6, for 20 to 30 minutes or until the topping is golden.
Serves 4

RAVIOLI WITH CHICKEN

125 g (4 oz) butter
1 small onion,
   chopped
50 g (2 oz) button
   mushrooms, diced
750 g (1½ lb) cooked
   chicken, minced
125 ml (4 fl oz) dry
   white wine
125 ml (4 fl oz)
   single cream
1 tablespoon chopped
   parsley
salt and pepper
500 g (1 lb) quantity
   pasta dough (see
   page 150)
1 beaten egg
4-6 tablespoons
   grated Parmesan
   cheese
parsley sprigs to
   garnish

Melt 25 g (1 oz) of the butter in a pan, add the onion and cook for 5 minutes, without browning. Add the mushrooms and cook for 2 minutes. Remove from the heat and stir in the chicken, wine, cream, parsley, and salt and pepper to taste. Leave until cold.

Cut the pasta in half. Cover with clingfilm and rest for 30 minutes. Roll out the pasta dough thinly.

Place teaspoons of the chicken mixture about 5 cm (2 inches) apart on one piece of pasta. Brush lightly with beaten egg between the filling.

Lay the second sheet of pasta lightly on top, pressing down between the filling to seal. Cut around the filling with a pastry wheel or knife to give little ravioli squares. Check that each ravioli is thoroughly sealed and place on a board to dry for 1 hour.

Cook until al dente. Transfer to a warmed serving dish with a slotted spoon. Add the remaining butter and toss well. Sprinkle with Parmesan cheese to taste and garnish with parsley. Serve immediately.
Serves 6

LEFT: *Ravioli with Chicken*

RIGHT: *Tagliatelle with Asparagus; Fettuccine with Courgettes*

TAGLIATELLE WITH ASPARAGUS

75 g (3 oz) butter
2 cloves garlic,
  crushed
500 g (1 lb) thin
  asparagus spears,
  cut into 2.5 cm
  (1 inch) lengths
284 ml (½ pint)
  carton double
  cream
1 tablespoon each
  chopped parsley
  and thyme
salt and pepper
500 g (1 lb) fresh
  tagliatelle
50 g (2 oz) Parmesan
  cheese, grated
thyme or parsley
  sprigs to garnish

Heat 50 g (2 oz) of the butter in a wok or frying pan, add the garlic and asparagus and cook gently, without browning, for 7 to 10 minutes, until the asparagus is just tender. Add the cream, herbs, and salt and pepper to taste. Remove from the heat.

Cook the pasta until *al dente*. Drain thoroughly and turn into a warmed serving dish. Add the remaining butter and toss well.

Return the sauce to the heat for 1 minute, then pour over the pasta. Sprinkle with the Parmesan cheese and garnish with thyme or parsley sprigs. Serve immediately.
Serves 6

FETTUCCINE WITH COURGETTES

750 g (1½ lb)
  courgettes
salt
50 g (2 oz) plain
  flour
oil for shallow frying
4 cloves garlic
500 g (1 lb) fresh
  fettuccine or fine
  noodles
50 g (2 oz) butter
12 basil leaves, torn
  into 2 or 3 pieces
50 g (2 oz) Parmesan
  cheese, grated
basil sprigs to garnish

Cut the courgettes into 5 cm (2 inch) lengths and arrange in layers in a colander, sprinkling each layer liberally with salt. Leave to drain for 1 to 2 hours. Rinse well and dry thoroughly on kitchen paper. Toss in the flour.

Heat the oil in a frying pan, add the whole garlic cloves and fry until coloured, then remove. Add the courgettes in batches and fry until golden. Drain on kitchen paper and keep hot.

Meanwhile, cook the pasta until *al dente*. Drain and turn into a warmed serving dish. Add the butter and basil and toss well. Stir in the courgettes, sprinkle with the cheese and garnish with basil. Serve immediately.
Serves 6

BAKED RIGATONI WITH MEAT SAUCE

2 tablespoons oil
50 g (2 oz) butter
1 onion, chopped
2 celery sticks,
    chopped
2 carrots, chopped
375 g (12 oz) minced
    beef
salt and pepper
300 ml (½ pint) dry
    white wine
6 tablespoons milk
little grated nutmeg
1-2 cloves garlic,
    crushed
1 × 397 g (14 oz)
    can tomatoes,
    chopped
500 g (1 lb) dried
    rigatoni or penne
40 g (1½ oz) butter
6 tablespoons grated
    Parmesan cheese
BECHAMEL SAUCE:
450 ml (¾ pint)
    milk
1 carrot
1 onion
3-4 peppercorns
1 bay leaf
50 g (2 oz) butter
50 g (2 oz) plain
    flour

Heat the oil and butter in a pan, add the onion, celery and carrots and cook for 2 minutes, without browning. Increase the heat, add the minced beef and brown well. Season liberally with salt and pepper, add the wine and cook rapidly until it has evaporated.

Lower the heat, add the milk and cook until it has reduced completely.

Stir in the nutmeg, garlic and tomatoes with their juice. Cover and simmer for 1 to 1½ hours, stirring occasionally. Check the seasoning.

Meanwhile, make the Béchamel sauce. Put the milk, carrot, onion, peppercorns and bay leaf in a pan and bring to the boil slowly. Turn off the heat, leave to cool, then strain.

Melt the butter in a pan, add the flour and cook for 1 minute, without browning. Gradually add the strained milk, stirring constantly. Bring to the boil and cook for 2 minutes. Season with salt and pepper to taste.

Cook the pasta until just *al dente*. Drain, place in a large bowl with the butter and toss well. Pour over the meat and Béchamel sauces, and 4 tablespoons of the Parmesan cheese; mix well.

Transfer to a buttered ovenproof dish, sprinkle with the remaining cheese and bake in a preheated moderately hot oven, 200°C (400°F), Gas Mark 6, for 20 to 25 minutes until hot and golden brown. Serve immediately.
Serves 6

MACARONI CHEESE

250 g (8 oz) dried
    short-cut macaroni
50 g (2 oz) butter
25 g (1 oz) plain
    flour
450 ml (¾ pint)
    milk
1 heaped teaspoon
    English mustard
dash of Tabasco sauce
dash of Worcester-
    shire sauce
175 g (6 oz) matured
    Cheddar cheese,
    grated
25 g (1 oz) dried
    breadcrumbs
25 g (1 oz) Parmesan
    cheese, grated
2 tomatoes, sliced

Cook the macaroni according to the packet instructions, drain thoroughly, then toss in half the butter.

Heat the remaining butter in a pan, stir in the flour and cook, stirring, for 2 minutes, without browning. Gradually add the milk and bring to the boil, stirring constantly. Cook for 2 minutes, then stir in the mustard, and Tabasco and Worcestershire sauces. Add the Cheddar cheese and stir until melted. Fold in the macaroni.

Spoon into a buttered ovenproof dish and sprinkle with the breadcrumbs and Parmesan cheese.

Bake in a preheated moderately hot oven, 200°C (400°F), Gas Mark 6, for 25 to 30 minutes. Arrange the tomato slices on top, return to the oven for 5 to 10 minutes, until hot and golden brown. Serve immediately.
Serves 4

ABOVE: *Macaroni Cheese*

RIGHT: *Noodles with Peppers; Pasta Turnovers*

NOODLES WITH PEPPERS

2 red peppers
250 g (8 oz)
    tomatoes
2 tablespoons oil
1 onion, chopped
salt and pepper
250 g (8 oz) Italian
    salami, chopped
250 g (8 oz) fresh
    egg tagliatelle
250 g (8 oz) fresh
    tagliatelle verdi
25 g (1 oz) butter
25 g (1 oz) Parmesan
    cheese, grated
    (optional)
TO GARNISH:
red pepper slices
thyme sprigs

Remove the core and seeds from the peppers. Peel thinly and cut into 1 cm (½ inch) squares. Skin, deseed and chop the tomatoes.

Heat the oil in a pan, add the onion and cook for 5 minutes, until golden brown, stirring. Lower heat, add the peppers and cook for 7 to 8 minutes, until soft, stirring occasionally.

Add the tomatoes and cook for 3 minutes. Season liberally with salt and pepper. Add the salami, check the seasoning and remove from the heat.

Meanwhile, cook the pasta until *al dente*. Drain thoroughly and turn into a warmed serving dish. Add the butter and toss well.

Return the sauce to the heat and boil for 1 minute. Pour over the pasta, sprinkle with the Parmesan cheese, if using, and garnish with pepper slices and thyme. Serve immediately.
Serves 6

PASTA TURNOVERS

500 g (1 lb) quantity
    pasta dough (see
    page 150)
750 g (1½ lb)
    spinach
25 g (1 oz) butter
1-2 cloves garlic,
    crushed
75 g (3 oz) full-fat
    soft cheese with
    garlic and herbs
pinch of grated
    nutmeg
1 tablespoon each
    chopped chives,
    parsley and
    marjoram
salt and pepper
a little beaten egg
oil for shallow frying
3-4 tablespoons
    grated Parmesan
    cheese to serve

Roll out the pasta dough very thinly, cover with clingfilm and leave to rest for 5 minutes.

Cook the spinach, with just the water clinging to the leaves after washing, for 3 minutes. Drain well and chop roughly.

Melt the butter in a frying pan, add the garlic and cook for 2 minutes, without browning. Stir in the spinach, cheese, nutmeg, herbs, salt to taste and lots of pepper.

Cut the pasta into 8 cm (3 inch) squares. Place a teaspoon of the filling in the centre of each square, brush the edges with beaten egg, fold over like a turnover and seal firmly. Place on a tea-towel to dry for 1 hour. Heat the oil in a frying pan, add a few turnovers at a time and fry for 3 minutes each side, until golden. Drain on kitchen paper.

Sprinkle with the Parmesan cheese and serve immediately.
Serves 6

BAKED MEAT LASAGNE

4 tablespoons olive oil
2 onions, chopped
3 cloves garlic, crushed
2 celery sticks, chopped
500 g (1 lb) minced beef
125 g (4 oz) chicken livers, chopped
salt and pepper
400 ml (15 fl oz) dry white wine
2 × 397 g (14 oz) cans tomatoes
½ teaspoon grated nutmeg
1 teaspoon dried mixed herbs
8 sheets no precook lasagne verdi
300 ml (½ pint) Béchamel Sauce (see page 152)
50 g (2 oz) Parmesan cheese, grated
25 g (1 oz) matured Cheddar cheese, grated
1 tablespoon dried breadcrumbs

Heat the oil in a large pan, add the onions and 2 cloves garlic and cook for 10 minutes, until pale golden. Stir in the celery and cook for 2 minutes.

Increase the heat and add the minced beef. Cook rapidly until lightly browned. Add the chicken livers, and season liberally with salt and pepper.

Pour over the wine, add the tomatoes with their juice, nutmeg and herbs. Bring to the boil, cover and simmer very gently for 2½ to 3 hours, stirring occasionally; if the mixture becomes too thick, add a little more wine. Stir in the remaining garlic and check the seasoning.

Spoon enough sauce into a large ovenproof dish or roasting tin to cover the base. Arrange some lasagne over this. Repeat the layers until all the sauce and lasagne are used, finishing with lasagne.

Spoon over Béchamel sauce and sprinkle with the cheeses and breadcrumbs.

Bake in a preheated moderately hot oven, 200°C (400°F), Gas Mark 6, for 45 to 50 minutes, until golden. Serve immediately.
Serves 6 to 8

SPAGHETTI CAROTESE

375 g (12 oz) dried spaghetti
5 tablespoons olive oil
6 carrots, thinly sliced
250 g (8 oz) tomatoes, skinned and chopped
3 tablespoons finely chopped fresh basil
salt and pepper
60 g (2½ oz) Parmesan cheese, grated

Cook the spaghetti in boiling salted water according to the packet instructions. Drain well and keep warm.

Meanwhile, heat half of the oil in a pan, add the carrots and cook, over a high heat, until just tender. Add the chopped tomatoes, basil and salt and pepper to taste, mixing well.

Add the cooked spaghetti and toss well to mix. Transfer to a heated serving dish and serve hot, sprinkled with the Parmesan cheese.
Serves 4

ABOVE: *Baked Meat Lasagne*

RIGHT: *Tortellini with Spinach and Herb Sauce*

PASTA STROGANOFF

25 g (1 oz) butter
1 onion, finely
    chopped
2 cloves garlic,
    crushed
250 g (8 oz)
    mushrooms, sliced
500 g (1 lb) lean
    minced beef
2 beef stock cubes
600 ml (1 pint)
    boiling water
2 tablespoons tomato
    purée
500 g (1 lb) dried
    penne
300 ml (½ pint)
    soured cream
salt and pepper
2 tablespoons
    chopped parsley

Melt the butter in a pan, add the onion and garlic and fry until softened, about 5 minutes. Add the mushrooms and cook for 1 minute. Crumble over the meat and cook, stirring frequently, until no longer pink. Add the crumbled stock cubes, water and tomato purée, mixing well. Bring to the boil, reduce the heat and simmer for 10 minutes.

Meanwhile cook the pasta in boiling salted water according to the packet instructions.

Stir the soured cream into the meat sauce and season with salt and pepper to taste.

Drain the pasta and divide between four warmed plates. Top with the sauce and serve. immediately, sprinkled with chopped parsley.

Serves 4

TORTELLINI WITH SPINACH AND HERB SAUCE

50 g (2 oz) butter
250 g (8 oz) frozen
    leaf spinach,
    thawed and
    chopped
pinch of grated
    nutmeg
salt and pepper
375 g (12 oz) fresh
    tortellini
125 g (4 oz) curd
    cheese
2 tablespoons single
    cream
2 teaspoons snipped
    chives
1 teaspoon chopped
    parsley
50 g (2 oz) Parmesan
    cheese, grated

Heat the butter in a large frying pan, add the spinach and toss thoroughly. Add the nutmeg and season to taste with salt and pepper. Cook for about 2 minutes, stirring constantly, until tender.

Meanwhile, cook the tortellini, according to the packet instructions, until just tender.

Stir in the curd cheese, cream, chives, parsley and half of the Parmesan cheese, then fold in the cooked spinach. Spoon into a heated serving dish and sprinkle with the remaining Parmesan cheese to serve.

Serves 4

RISOTTO WITH MEAT SAUCE

1.2 litres (2 pints) chicken stock (approximately)
1 tablespoon oil
50 g (2 oz) butter
1 onion, finely chopped
375 g (12 oz) Italian risotto rice
25 g (1 oz) grated Parmesan cheese
salt and pepper
Chicken Liver Sauce or Meat Sauce (see page 154)

Place the stock in a saucepan and bring to simmering point.

Heat the oil and half the butter in a heavy-based saucepan, add the onion and fry gently until soft and golden. Add the rice and cook, stirring, for 1 minute until translucent.

Add the stock a little at a time, adding more as each addition is absorbed and stirring frequently. Cook until the rice is just tender and the consistency creamy, about 10 minutes. Stir in the remaining butter, the cheese, and salt and pepper to taste.

Turn onto a warmed serving dish and pour the sauce into the centre. Serve with extra Parmesan cheese.
Serves 4

COUNTRY-STYLE RISOTTO

3 tablespoons olive oil
1 onion, chopped
2 celery sticks, thinly sliced
125 g (4 oz) courgettes, thinly sliced
125 g (4 oz) shelled peas or broad beans
375 g (12 oz) Italian risotto rice
1.2 litres (2 pints) chicken stock (approximately)
25 g (1 oz) butter
125 g (4 oz) cooked ham, cut into strips
25-50 g (1-2 oz) grated Parmesan
salt and pepper

Heat the oil in a heavy-based saucepan, add the onion and celery and fry gently for 3 minutes. Stir in the courgettes and peas or beans, cover and cook gently for 5 minutes. Add the rice and cook, stirring for 1 minute until translucent.

Add the stock, a little at a time, adding more as each addition is absorbed and stirring frequently. Cook until the rice is just tender and the consistency creamy, about 10 minutes. Stir in the butter, ham, cheese, and salt and pepper to taste.

Turn onto a warmed serving dish and serve immediately, with extra Parmesan cheese.
Serves 4

SPAGHETTI WITH TOMATO AND CHEESE SAUCE

1 kg (2 lb) tomatoes
1 celery stick
1 carrot, chopped
2 onions, chopped
150 ml (1/4 pint) dry white wine
2 tablespoons chopped marjoram
25 g (1 oz) matured Cheddar cheese, grated
2 tablespoons grated Parmesan cheese
salt and pepper
500 g (1 lb) fresh spaghetti
25 g (1 oz) butter

Roughly chop the tomatoes and celery and place in a pan with the carrot and onions. Bring slowly to the boil, cover and simmer for 30 minutes. Rub through a sieve and return to the pan.

Add the wine, bring to the boil and cook for 15 to 20 minutes, until the sauce has reduced and thickened. Remove from the heat and stir in the marjoram, cheeses, and salt and pepper to taste.

Cook the spaghetti until al dente. Drain thoroughly and turn into a warmed serving dish. Add the butter and toss well. Heat the sauce thoroughly and pour over the pasta.
Serves 6

MARINATED PASTA AND MUSHROOMS

175 g (6 oz) dried penne
375 g (12 oz) button mushrooms
6 large spring onions, chopped
1 tablespoon chopped fresh thyme
200 ml (7 fl oz) grape juice
250 g (8 oz) white seedless grapes, halved
salt and pepper

Cook the pasta in boiling salted water according to the packet instructions. Drain well and allow to cool.

Place the mushrooms, spring onions and thyme in a large bowl and pour over the grape juice. Mix well, cover and chill for about 3 hours, stirring occasionally.

Add the grapes, pasta and salt and pepper to taste, mixing well. Serve lightly chilled.
Serves 4 to 6

LEFT: *Risotto with Meat Sauce; Country-Style Risotto*

RIGHT: *Risotto*

RISOTTO

50 g (2 oz) streaky bacon, derinded and chopped
1 onion, chopped
1 celery stick, chopped
1/2 green pepper, cored, deseeded and chopped
1/2 red pepper, cored, deseeded and chopped
25 g (1 oz) butter
250 g (8 oz) long-grain rice
375 g (12 oz) cooked chicken, chopped
600 ml (1 pint) chicken stock
salt and pepper
1 teaspoon dried thyme or parsley
2 tablespoons grated Parmesan cheese

Place the bacon in a pan and fry very gently until the fat runs. Then add the onion, celery and peppers and fry gently until soft stirring occasionally. Remove the bacon and vegetables from the pan, drain on kitchen paper.

Melt the butter in the same pan and add the rice. Fry for 2 to 3 minutes, stirring to prevent sticking, until the fat is absorbed, then stir in the bacon, vegetables, chicken and stock. Bring to the boil, reduce the heat, cover and simmer for 20 minutes or until the rice is tender and all the liquid has been absorbed.

Add salt and pepper to taste and stir in the herbs. Sprinkle the risotto with Parmesan cheese, and serve immediately, while still piping hot.
Serves 4

LASAGNE WITH MEAT SAUCE

butter
450 ml (¾ pint) Rich
    Meat Sauce (see
    page 155)
175 g (6 oz) no
    precook lasagne
    verdi
600 ml (1 pint)
    Béchamel Sauce
    (see page 152)
40 g (1½ oz) grated
    Parmesan cheese

Butter a 20 cm (8 inch) square ovenproof dish, at least 4 cm (1½ inches) deep. Spread a layer of Rich meat sauce on the bottom, cover with a layer of lasagne, then a layer of Rich meat sauce and finish with a thin layer of Béchamel sauce and a sprinkling of cheese. Repeat these layers twice more, finishing with cheese.

Bake in a preheated moderately hot oven, 200°C (400°F), Gas Mark 6, for 20 to 25 minutes, until golden and bubbling. Serve immediately.
Serves 4 to 6

PASTA WITH CHICKEN LIVERS

1 tablespoon oil
50 g (2 oz) butter
4 shallots, chopped
4 rashers back bacon,
    derinded and
    chopped
250 g (8 oz) minced
    beef
150 ml (¼ pint) each
    dry Vermouth and
    dry white wine
375 g (12 oz)
    tomatoes, skinned
    deseeded and
    chopped
salt and pepper
2 cloves garlic,
    crushed
2 tablespoons each
    chopped parsley,
    marjoram and sage
250 g (8 oz) chicken
    livers, chopped
500 g (1 lb) dried
    fusilli or conchiglie

Heat the oil and half the butter in a pan, add the shallots and cook, stirring constantly, for 2 to 3 minutes, without browning. Add the bacon and minced beef, increase the heat and brown quickly, stirring.

Add the Vermouth and wine and boil rapidly for 15 minutes. Stir in the tomatoes and season well with salt and pepper. Stir in the garlic and herbs. Add the chicken livers and cook for 3 minutes.

Cook the pasta according to the packet instructions. Drain thoroughly, turn into a warmed serving dish, add the remaining butter and toss well.

Spoon the sauce over the pasta and toss well. Serve immediately.
Serves 6

ITALIAN FOCACCIA BREAD

It is mistakenly though that the Italians eat pasta at every meal. Not true, but they do eat a surprising amount of bread. Rarely is a table laid without its bread accompaniment. There are many types of Italian bread from the plain rustic to the elaborate fancy, but perhaps the most popular is Focaccia. This is a rustic Italian flat bread, made with olive oil and dusted with crushed rock salt. Normally it is served plain to accompany antipasti, main courses and cheeses but it is also frequently found topped with onion, olives, cheese and herbs for special meal occasions. Focaccia bread can now be found ready-made in many stores and both types make a wonderful accompaniment to soup.

LEFT: *Pasta with Chicken Livers*

RIGHT: *Cannelloni*

PASTA AND SPINACH ROLL

75 g (3 oz) butter
1 large onion,
    chopped
50 g (2 oz) Parma
    ham, diced
500 g (1 lb) frozen
    leaf spinach,
    thawed, drained
    and roughly
    chopped
200 g (7 oz) Ricotta
    or curd cheese
65 g (2½ oz)
    Parmesan cheese,
    grated
little grated nutmeg
1 egg yolk
250 g (8 oz) quantity
    pasta dough (see
    page 150)
300 ml (½ pint)
    Béchamel Sauce
    (see page 152)
fresh herbs to garnish
TOMATO SAUCE:
1 tablespoon olive oil
1 large onion, finely
    chopped
2 carrots, chopped
2 celery sticks,
    chopped
1 × 397 g (14 oz)
    can chopped
    tomatoes
150 ml (¼ pint) dry
    white wine
½ teaspoon dried
    mixed herbs
salt and pepper

First make the tomato sauce. Heat the olive oil in a pan, add the onion, carrots and celery and cook for 5 minutes, without browning, stirring occasionally. Add the tomatoes and their juice, the wine, herbs, and salt and pepper to taste. Bring to the boil, cover and simmer for 20 minutes. Remove the lid and cook for 10 to 15 minutes until thickened; set aside.

Melt the butter in a pan, add the onion and cook until golden brown. Lower the heat, stir in the ham and spinach and cook for 5 minutes, stirring occasionally.

Put the Ricotta or curd cheese and all but 2 tablespoons of the Parmesan cheese in a bowl. Stir in the spinach mixture, and season with salt and pepper to taste. Add the nutmeg and egg yolk.

Roll out the pasta to an oblong shape and cover with the filling, leaving a 2.5 cm (1 inch) border around the edge. Fold in the two ends and roll up like a Swiss roll. Wrap in muslin and tie the ends securely with string.

Cook in boiling salted water for 20 minutes. Remove from the pan, leave to cool then remove the muslin.

Stir the Béchamel sauce into the tomato sauce.

Slice the roll into 15 mm (⅝ inch) thick slices and arrange in a buttered ovenproof dish. Spoon over the sauce and sprinkle with the reserved Parmesan cheese.

Bake uncovered in a preheated moderately hot oven, 200°C (400°F), Gas Mark 6, for 15 to 20 minutes. Garnish with fresh herbs if liked, and serve immediately.

Serves 4 to 6
NOTE: if you do not have a large enough pan, make 2 smaller rolls.

CANNELLONI

450 ml (¾ pint)
    Béchamel Sauce
    (see page 152)
12 tubes cannelloni
300 ml (½ pint)
    Speedy Tomato
    Sauce (see page
    155)
salt and pepper
3 tablespoons grated
    Parmesan cheese
25 g (1 oz) butter
FILLING:
2 tablespoons oil
1 onion, chopped
1 clove garlic, crushed
250 g (8 oz) minced
    beef
250 g (8 oz) frozen
    chopped spinach,
    cooked and
    squeezed dry
40 g (1½ oz) grated
    Parmesan cheese
1 egg yolk

To prepare the filling, heat the oil in a saucepan, add the onion and garlic and fry gently until soft. Add the meat and cook, stirring, until well browned. Stir in the remaining ingredients. Bind the mixture with 2 tablespoons of the Béchamel sauce and season well with salt and pepper.

Fill the cannelloni tubes with the meat mixture and place in a buttered 20 cm (8 inch) square ovenproof dish.

Pour over the Speedy tomato sauce and cover with the Béchamel sauce. Sprinkle with cheese and dot with butter.

Bake in a moderately hot oven, 200°C (400°F), Gas Mark 6, for 15 to 20 minutes, until golden and bubbling.

Serves 4 to 6

TAGLIATELLE AND SWEETCORN

250 g (8 oz) dried
    egg tagliatelle
salt and pepper
15 g (½ oz) butter
1 tablespoon oil
1 onion, sliced
1 × 326 g (11 oz)
    can sweetcorn
2 × 19 g (¾ oz)
    packets white
    sauce mix
150 ml (¼ pint) milk
1 teaspoon anchovy
    essence
1 teaspoon
    Worcestershire
    sauce
TO GARNISH:
chopped parsley
chopped hazelnuts

Cook the tagliatelle in boiling, salted water according to the packet instructions. Drain thoroughly and transfer to a warmed serving dish; keep hot.

Melt the butter and oil in the pan, add the onion and fry gently for 2 to 3 minutes. Add the drained corn and salt and pepper to taste and heat through.

Make up the white sauce mix with the milk, as directed on the packet. Add the anchovy essence and Worcestershire sauce.

When the corn mixture is hot, pour over the tagliatelle with three-quarters of the sauce and toss well. Top with the reserved sauce and garnish with parsley and nuts.
Serves 4

TAGLIATELLE BOLOGNAISE

375 g (12 oz) dried
    tagliatelle
salt
25 g (1 oz) butter
450 ml (¾ pint) hot
    Rich Meat Sauce
    (see page 155)
2 tablespoons grated
    Parmesan cheese

Cook the tagliatelle in boiling salted water according to the packet instructions. Drain thoroughly.

Melt the butter and pour into a deep serving dish, add 4 tablespoons of the Rich meat sauce, the pasta and Parmesan cheese. Toss lightly until the pasta is coated. Pile the remaining sauce on top and hand more cheese separately.
Serves 4

LEFT: *Tagliatelle and Sweetcorn; Vegetable and Walnut Lasagne*

RIGHT: *Pasta Jumble*

VEGETABLE AND WALNUT LASAGNE

750 g (1½ lb)
  parsnips, chopped
salt and pepper
25 g (1 oz) butter
2 tablespoons
  chopped parsley
6 sheets of no precook
  lasagne
340 g (12 oz) carton
  cottage cheese
500 g (1 lb) frozen
  chopped spinach,
  thawed and
  drained
¼ teaspoon grated
  nutmeg
50 g (2 oz)
  Emmental, sliced
25 g (1 oz) walnuts,
  roughly chopped
1 large tomato, sliced
  and halved
parsley to garnish

Cook the parsnips in boiling salted water in a 1.75 litre (3 pint) shallow flameproof dish for 12 to 15 minutes or until tender. Drain and mash in the dish with half the butter and the parsley.

Cover with half the lasagne, then the cottage cheese, then the remaining lasagne. Cover with the spinach and season with the nutmeg, salt and pepper to taste. Arrange the cheese slices along 2 sides of the dish.

Cook in a preheated moderate oven, 180°C (350°F), Gas Mark 4, for 30 minutes. Sprinkle the walnuts down the centre and dot with the remaining butter. Arrange the tomato slices on either side of the walnuts.

Garnish with parsley and serve hot with crusty bread.
Serves 4

FUSILLI WITH TUNA TOMATO SAUCE

500 g (1 lb) dried
  fusilli
1 tablespoon oil
1 onion, chopped
3 celery sticks, sliced
1 tablespoon plain
  flour
150 ml (¼ pint)
  vegetable stock
230 g (8 oz) can
  chopped tomatoes
2 tablespoons tomato
  chutney
198 g (7 oz) can tuna,
  drained and flaked
50 g (2 oz) Cheddar
  cheese, grated

Cook the pasta in boiling salted water, according to the packet instructions, until just tender.

Meanwhile, heat the oil in a pan, add the onion and celery and cook until softened, about 8 minutes. Add the flour and cook for 1 minute. Gradually stir in the stock then add the tomtoes and chutney, mixing well. Bring to the boil, stirring constantly. Reduce the heat, add the tuna and cook for 1 minute.

Drain the pasta and place in a heated serving dish. Spoon over the sauce and sprinkle with the cheese.
Serves 4

PASTA JUMBLE

125 g (4 oz) dried
  pasta shapes
salt and pepper
25 g (1 oz) butter or
  margarine
25 g (1 oz) flour
300 ml (½ pint)
  milk
½ teaspoon mustard
125 g (4 oz) Double
  Gloucester cheese,
  grated
125 g (4 oz) lean
  ham, chopped
1 green pepper cored,
  deseeded and
  chopped
2 oz (50 g) sweetcorn
TO GARNISH:
1 tomato, sliced
parsley sprig

Cook the pasta in plenty of boiling salted water according to the packet instructions, then rinse and drain.

Melt the butter or margarine in a pan, stir in the flour and cook for 1 minute. Remove from the heat and gradually blend in the milk. Heat, stirring continuously until the sauce thickens. Add salt and pepper to taste, and the mustard; cook for 1 minute.

Stir in the pasta, cheese, ham, green pepper and sweetcorn, mix well and transfer to a shallow ovenproof dish. Place in a preheated moderately hot oven, 190°C (375°F), Gas Mark 5, for 20 minutes.

Garnish with tomato slices and parsley
Serves 4

VEGETABLES AND SALADS

The Italian cook and housewife demands the very best quality vegetable and salad ingredients – not surprising, since so many of them are served raw.

Boiled, sautéed, steamed, dressed or marinated vegetables are served at almost every course including antipasti; first pasta, rice or soup courses, as an accompaniment to, or as a main component of, the second meat, poultry or fish course; and, naturally, the salad course.

Fortunately the selection of vegetables is vast and the quality exceptional. Classic and inspirational recipes make the best use of shiny peppers in traffic light colours; luscious tomatoes; tender courgettes; crisp, crunchy and piquant chicory; mushrooms from the simple to the sophisticated and unusual; beans in all their glory, that we seldom see fresh; and spinach, so versatile in salads, stuffings, sauces and pasta.

For healthy offerings remember to cook vegetables for the minimum amount of time, as stated, in a small amount of water to preserve the nutrients. And take a tip from the Italian housewife who never throws away the cooking liquid but uses it in soups, stews and sauces.

AVOCADO AND MUSHROOM SALAD

250 g (8 oz) button
    mushrooms, sliced
½ head of frisée
1 lime or lemon
2 large avocado pears
25 g (1 oz) pine
    kernels, toasted
DRESSING:
6 tablespoons olive
    oil
3-4 tablespoons lime
    juice
1 teaspoon finely
    grated lemon rind
1 clove garlic, crushed
1 teaspoon crushed
    coriander seeds
1 teaspoon honey
salt and pepper

Mix the dressing ingredients together, seasoning with salt and pepper to taste. Put the mushrooms in a large bowl, pour over the dressing and toss well, until all the mushrooms are coated.

Arrange the frisée on a flat plate. Squeeze the juice from half of the lime or lemon; slice the remainder. Slice the avocados and sprinkle with the lime or lemon juice to prevent browning. Arrange on top of the frisée.

Spoon the mushrooms on to the centre. Sprinkle the pine kernels over the salad, and garnish with the lime or lemon slices. Serve immediately.
Serves 4

COUNTRY GARDEN SALAD

250 g (8 oz) very
    small new potatoes
salt and pepper
mint sprig
250 g (8 oz) carrots,
    quartered
    lengthways
250 g (8 oz) peas
125 g (4 oz) small
    green beans
1 thin leek, sliced
DRESSING:
4 tablespoons oil
2 tablespoons lemon
    juice
1 teaspoon mustard
½ teaspoon clear
    honey
1 clove garlic, crushed
2 tablespoons
    chopped mint

Cook the potatoes in boiling salted water with a sprig of mint for 10 to 12 minutes, until tender. Drain and cool under running cold water. Drain thoroughly.

Cook the carrots in boiling salted water for 7 to 10 minutes, add the peas and beans to the pan and cook for a further 3 minutes. Drain the vegetables and cool under running cold water. Drain thoroughly.

Put the cooked vegetables in a large bowl and add the leek.

Mix the dressing ingredients together, seasoning with salt and pepper to taste. Spoon over the vegetables and mix well.

Pile the salad into a salad bowl and serve immediately.
Serves 4

MOZZARELLA SALAD

3 large tomatoes
¼ cucumber
1 red and 1 green
　pepper, cored and
　deseeded
2-3 courgettes
250 g (8 oz)
　Mozzarella cheese
4 spring onions,
　chopped
DRESSING:
6 tablespoons olive
　oil
3-4 tablespoons lime
　juice
1-2 cloves garlic,
　crushed
1 teaspoon each clear
　honey and French
　mustard
1 tablespoon each
　chopped parsley,
　basil and marjoram
1-2 teaspoons green
　peppercorns
salt
TO GARNISH:
basil sprigs

Thinly slice the tomatoes, cucumber, peppers, courgettes and cheese and arrange on a flat serving platter. Sprinkle with the spring onions.

Mix the dressing ingredients together, seasoning with salt to taste. Spoon over the salad, cover and chill for 30 minutes. Remove from the refrigerator 15 minutes before required.

Garnish with basil sprigs to serve.
Serves 4 to 6

Mozzarella Salad

POTATO AND DILL SALAD

1 kg (2 lb) new
　potatoes
salt and pepper
6 spring onions
7 tablespoons
　mayonnaise
good pinch of chilli
　powder
1 bunch of dill,
　roughly chopped
2 tablespoons
　sunflower seeds,
　toasted
dill sprigs to garnish

Cook the potatoes in boiling salted water for 15 minutes, until tender. Drain and cool, then slice them into a bowl.

Chop the spring onions into 2.5 cm (1 inch) pieces and add to the bowl with the mayonnaise and chilli powder. Season with salt and pepper to taste. Stir in the dill.

Transfer to a serving dish and sprinkle with the sunflower seeds. Garnish with dill to serve.
Serves 10

LEFT: *Avocado and Mushroom Salad; Country Garden Salad*

FRISÉE AND BACON SALAD

175 g (6 oz) streaky
　bacon, derinded
3 thick slices stale
　bread
oil for deep-frying
1 head of frisée
2 heads of radicchio
1-2 avocado pears
juice of 1 lemon
1-2 hard-boiled eggs
1 tablespoon chopped
　parsley to garnish
DRESSING:
6 tablespoons olive
　oil
3 tablespoons lemon
　juice
1-2 teaspoons coarse
　grain mustard
1-2 cloves garlic,
　crushed
1 teaspoon honey
salt and pepper

Grill the bacon until crisp and golden brown, cool and crumble into pieces.

Remove the crusts, then cut the bread into cubes or rounds. Heat the oil in a pan, add the croûtons and fry until golden brown. Drain on kitchen paper.

Separate the frisée and radicchio into leaves, tear into pieces and place in a deep bowl. Roughly chop the avocado and toss in the lemon juice. Drain and add to the salad with the bacon and croûtons.

Chop the egg white, sieve the yolk, and sprinkle over the salad.

Mix the dressing ingredients together, seasoning with salt and pepper to taste, pour over the salad and toss well. Sprinkle with the parsley and serve immediately.
Serves 4

BROAD BEAN AND FENNEL SALAD

1.5 kg (3½ lb)
  shelled broad beans
6 spring onions,
  chopped
4 bulbs of fennel,
  chopped
1 stick celery, chopped
juice of 2 lemons
50 g (2 oz) flaked
  almonds, toasted
DRESSING:
2-3 cloves garlic,
  crushed
pinch of cayenne
3 × 150 g (5 oz)
  cartons yogurt
4 tablespoons
  chopped mint
grated rind of 2 limes
TO GARNISH:
fennel leaves

Cook the beans in boiling salted water for 5 minutes, until just tender. Drain and cool under cold running water. Drain thoroughly and place in a large bowl. Add the spring onions. Toss the fennel and celery in the lemon juice and add both to the beans.

Mix the dressing ingredients together, spoon over the salad and toss well.

Pile into a serving dish, sprinkle with the almonds and garnish with fennel leaves if liked.

Serves 20

ITALIAN RICE SALAD

1 chicken carcass
1 bouquet garni
1 large onion
750 g (1½ lb)
  American long-
  grain rice
150 ml (¼ pint) dry
  white wine
salt and pepper
2 each red, green and
  yellow peppers,
  cored, deseeded and
  chopped
250 g (8 oz)
  tomatoes, deseeded
  and chopped
250 g (8 oz) Italian
  salami, diced
8 basil and 8 oregano
  sprigs, chopped
125 g (4 oz) cashew
  nuts
Dressing:
2 teaspoons Dijon
  mustard
6 tablespoons red
  wine vinegar
12 tablespoons olive
  oil
4 cloves garlic,
  crushed
3 teaspoons clear
  honey

Put the chicken carcass in a large pan of cold water with the bouquet garni and onion. Bring to the boil, cover and simmer for 1 to 1½ hours. Strain, reserving the stock. Remove any meat from the bones, chop and set aside.

Place the rice, reserved stock, wine, and salt to taste in a large pan and cook for 12 to 15 minutes, until tender. Drain off any remaining liquid and cool.

Place the rice in a large bowl and stir in the chopped chicken meat.

Mix the dressing ingredients together, seasoning with salt and pepper to taste. Pour over the rice and mix well.

Fold in the remaining ingredients and transfer to a serving dish.

Serves 20

SALAD DRESSING

A well made salad dressing can transform a good salad into something really exciting, but it is most important to use good ingredients. Olive oil is considered superior to other oils for dressings and the Italians use it liberally. For a basic dressing put 175 ml (6 fl oz) olive oil, 4 tablespoons wine vinegar, 1 teaspoon mustard, 1 crushed clove garlic, 1 teaspoon clear honey and seasoning to taste in a jar and shake. For a ginger dressing add 1 tablespoon chopped fresh root ginger.

LEFT: *Broad Bean and Fennel Salad*

RIGHT: *Winter Salad; Green Salad with Noodles*

WINTER SALAD

500 g (1 lb) dried
 tagliatelle verdi
4 celery sticks
1 red pepper
4 red dessert apples
juice of 1 lemon
1/4-1/2 green or white
 cabbage, shredded
125 g (4 oz) black
 olives
25 g (1 oz) gherkins,
 sliced
DRESSING:
4-6 tablespoons
 mayonnaise
2 tablespoons French
 mustard
1 teaspoon lemon
 juice
1 clove garlic, crushed
2 tablespoons each
 chopped parsley
 and chives
1-2 tablespoons
 capers, drained

Cook the tagliatelle according to the packet instructions. Drain and cool quickly under cold running water. Drain thoroughly and place in a large bowl.

Slice the celery and core, deseed and slice the red pepper. Add to the tagliatelle.

Core and slice the apples and toss in the lemon juice. Add to the salad with the cabbage.

Mix the dressing ingredients together and carefully mix into the salad with the olives and gherkins.

Transfer to a serving dish and serve immediately.
Serves 4 to 8

GREEN SALAD WITH NOODLES

150 ml (1/4 pint) oil
500 g (1 lb) fresh
 tagliatelle
125 g (4 oz) streaky
 bacon, derinded
1/2 head of frisée
1 Cos lettuce
250 g (8 oz) spinach
1 bunch of watercress
1 bunch of spring
 onions, sliced
2 avocado pears
1 hard-boiled egg
DRESSING:
6 tablespoons oil
3 tablespoons lemon
 juice
1-2 cloves garlic,
 crushed
1/2 teaspoon tarragon
 or herb mustard
1 teaspoon honey
1 tablespoon each
 chopped marjoram,
 parsley and thyme

Heat the oil in a wok or large frying pan, add the noodles in batches and fry until golden. Drain on kitchen paper and set aside.

Fry the bacon in its own fat until crisp. Crumble and set aside.

Tear the frisée, lettuce and spinach leaves into pieces and place in a deep serving bowl with the watercress and spring onions. Slice the avocados and add to the bowl with the noodles.

Mix the dressing ingredients together, pour over the salad and toss well.

Chop the egg white and sieve the yolk and sprinkle over the salad with the bacon. Serve immediately.
Serves 4 to 6

BEAN AND HAZELNUT SALAD

500 g (1 lb) green beans
salt and pepper
50 g (2 oz) shelled hazelnuts
few lettuce leaves
fresh herbs to garnish (optional)
DRESSING:
1 teaspoon Dijon mustard
finely grated rind of ½ lemon
juice of 1 lemon
7-8 tablespoons double cream, lightly whipped

Cook the beans in boiling salted water for 4 to 5 minutes, until just tender. Drain, cool under cold running water. Drain thoroughly. Cut the hazelnuts into thin slices. Place under a moderate grill until golden.

Mix the dressing ingredients together in a large bowl, add the beans and toss well. Season with salt and pepper to taste.

Arrange the lettuce on a serving dish. Pile the beans in the centre and sprinkle over the nuts. Garnish with fresh herbs as liked, and serve immediately.
Serves 4

COURGETTE AND BACON SALAD

500 g (1 lb) baby courgettes
2 spring onions
175 g (6 oz) streaky bacon, derinded
2 hard-boiled egg yolks, sieved
DRESSING:
6 tablespoons olive oil
3 tablespoons lemon juice
1 teaspoon clear honey
1 teaspoon coarse-grain mustard
1-2 cloves garlic, crushed
2 tablespoons each chopped marjoram and thyme
salt and pepper
TO GARNISH:
marjoram and thyme sprigs

Slice the courgettes very thinly and arrange on a plate. Chop the spring onions finely and sprinkle on top.

Mix the dressing ingredients together, seasoning with salt and pepper to taste. Spoon over the courgettes and set aside.

Grill the bacon until crisp and golden brown, cool and crumble into pieces.

Sprinkle the egg yolk and bacon over the salad, garnish with marjoram and thyme sprigs and serve immediately.
Serves 4

CONTINENTAL SUMMER SALAD

4 carrots, grated
1 tablespoon chopped parsley
2 small fennel bulbs, sliced
juice of ½ lemon
1 tablespoon chopped thyme
2 large tomatoes
125 g (4 oz) Mozzarella cheese
175 g (6 oz) spinach
1 head of radicchio
50 g (2 oz) salted cashew nuts
DRESSING:
6 tablespoons olive oil
3 tablespoons lemon juice
1 teaspoon each grated lemon rind, French mustard and clear honey
1-2 cloves garlic, crushed
3 tablespoons chopped basil
salt and pepper

Mix together the carrots and parsley and set aside.

Mix the fennel, lemon juice and thyme together.

Arrange the carrots on one quarter of a large platter, the fennel on the next quarter.

Slice the tomatoes and Mozzarella and arrange alternately in the third quarter.

Tear the spinach and radicchio leaves into pieces and arrange on the remaining quarter of the platter. Sprinkle with the nuts.

Mix the dressing ingredients together, seasoning with salt and pepper to taste. Spoon over the salad and serve immediately.
Serves 4
NOTE: This dish is also suitable to serve as an hors d'oeuvre.

Bean and Hazelnut Salad; Continental Summer Salad; Courgette and Bacon Salad

Herby Macaroni Salad

CHICORY, ORANGE AND WALNUT SALAD

2 heads of chicory
3 tablespoons virgin
    olive oil
1 tablespoon lemon
    juice
salt and pepper
3 oranges, peeled,
    pith removed and
    cut into large
    chunks
50 g (2 oz) walnuts,
    chopped

Separate the leaves from one head of the chicory, wash, dry then arrange on a flat serving dish. Slice the remaining head coarsely, wash and drain thoroughly.

Beat the oil with the lemon juice and salt and pepper to taste. Add the orange chunks, sliced chicory and chopped walnuts. Toss well to mix then spoon over the chicory leaves. Serve as soon as possible.
Serves 4

CAPONATA

1 large aubergine
salt and pepper
2 celery sticks, sliced
3 tablespoons olive
    oil
1 onion, chopped
1 × 227 g (8 oz) can
    tomatoes, drained
    and chopped
1½ teaspoons tomato
    purée
40 g (1½ oz) green
    olives, pitted
1 tablespoon wine
    vinegar
1½ teaspoons soft
    brown sugar
1 tablespoon capers
few lettuce leaves

Cut the aubergine into 1 cm (½ inch) cubes. Place in a colander, sprinkle with salt and leave for 30 minutes. Rinse and dry with kitchen paper.

Blanch the celery in boiling water for 5 minutes; drain.

Heat 2 tablespoons of the oil in a heavy-based pan, add the aubergines and fry for 10 to 15 minutes, stirring frequently, until beginning to turn golden. Remove from the pan.

Add the remaining oil to the pan and fry the onion gently for 5 minutes, until softened. Add the tomatoes, tomato purée, olives, celery, and salt and pepper to taste. Cover and simmer for 5 minutes.

Add the vinegar, sugar, capers and aubergine, cover and simmer for 5 minutes; leave to cool. Serve on individual dishes lined with the lettuce leaves.
Serves 4 to 5

HERBY MACARONI SALAD

500 g (1 lb) dried
    short-cut macaroni
1 red pepper, cored,
    deseeded and diced
½ cucumber, diced
150 g (5 oz) carton
    natural yogurt
1-2 cloves garlic,
    crushed
1 tablespoon each
    chopped parsley,
    basil, thyme,
    tarragon and chives
175 g (6 oz) streaky
    bacon, derinded
50 g (2 oz) peanuts
TO GARNISH:
herb sprigs

Cook the macaroni according to packet instructions. Drain and cool quickly under running cold water. Drain thoroughly and place in a large bowl. Stir in the red pepper, cucumber, yogurt, garlic and herbs. Transfer to a salad bowl.

Fry the bacon in its own fat until crisp, then chop into pieces and sprinkle over the salad with the peanuts.

Garnish with herbs sprigs if liked, and serve immediately.
Serves 4 to 6

TUNA AND BEAN SALAD

1 × 432 g (15 oz)
    can red kidney
    beans
1 × 432 g (15 oz)
    can cannellini
    beans
2-3 celery sticks
2-3 large spring
    onions
2 heads of radicchio
1 × 198 g (7 oz) can
    tuna fish, drained
    and flaked
1 bunch watercress
2 large slices bread
oil for deep-frying
DRESSING:
6 tablespoons olive
    oil
3 tablespoons lime or
    lemon juice
1-2 cloves garlic,
    crushed
1 teaspoon honey
2 tablespoons snipped
    chives
2 tablespoons
    chopped parsley
salt and pepper

Drain the beans, rinse in a colander under cold running water and drain well. Place in a bowl.

Thinly slice the celery, chop the spring onions, and tear the radicchio leaves into pieces. Add to the beans with the tuna fish.

Mix the dressing ingredients together, seasoning with salt and pepper to taste. Pour over the salad and mix well.

Arrange the watercress in a serving dish and spoon the salad into the centre.

Remove the crusts and cut the bread into cubes or crescent shapes, using small cutters. Heat the oil in a pan, add the croûtons and fry until golden. Drain on kitchen paper. Sprinkle over the salad and serve immediately.

Serves 4

MOZZARELLA AND TOMATO SALAD

500 g (1 lb) large
    tomatoes, sliced
salt and pepper
250 g (8 oz)
    Mozzarella
    cheese, sliced
3 tablespoons olive
    oil
2 tablespoons each
    chopped parsley
    and basil

Layer the tomatoes in a shallow serving dish, sprinkling each layer with salt and pepper. Arrange the Mozzarella in overlapping layers on top of the tomatoes. Pour over the oil and sprinkle with the herbs.

Serve with a green salad, salami if liked, and granary bread.

Serves 4

FENNEL AND PASTA SALAD

500 g (1 lb) conchiglie
3 large fennel bulbs,
    sliced
2-3 red apples,
    cored and sliced
juice of 1 lemon
4 spring onions
4 tomatoes
2 tablespoons sesame
    seeds, toasted
50 g (2 oz) salted
    cashew nuts
DRESSING:
6 tablespoons oil
3 tablespoons lemon
    juice
1 teaspoon each
    French mustard
    and clear honey
TO GARNISH:
fennel leaves

Cook the pasta according to the packet instructions. Drain and cool quickly under cold running water. Drain thoroughly and place in a large bowl.

Toss the fennel and apples in the lemon juice, then add to the pasta. Chop the spring onions and skin, deseed and chop the tomatoes. Add to the pasta.

Mix the dressing ingredients together and pour over the salad. Transfer to a serving bowl. Sprinkle with the sesame seeds and cashew nuts and garnish with fennel leaves, if liked. Serve immediately.

Serves 4 to 6

Fennel and Pasta Salad

Tagliatelle Salad

TAGLIATELLE SALAD

500 g (1 lb) fresh
　tagliatelle
2 × 432 g (15 oz)
　cans red kidney
　beans
2 × 198 g (7 oz) cans
　tuna fish
4 young courgettes
50 g (2 oz)
　mushrooms
2 small leeks or
　spring onions
1 tablespoon green
　peppercorns
DRESSING:
4 tablespoons
　mayonnaise
2 tablespoons each
　chopped parsley
　and chives
2 teaspoons lemon
　juice
1 teaspoon finely
　grated lemon rind
chilli powder
salt
TO GARNISH:
mint sprigs (optional)
lemon slices

Cook the tagliatelle until *al dente*. Drain and cool quickly under cold running water. Drain thoroughly and place in a large bowl.

Rinse and drain the kidney beans under cold running water. Drain and flake the tuna. Thinly slice the courgettes and mushrooms; chop the spring onions. Add to the pasta with the peppercorns.

Mix the dressing ingredients together, seasoning with chilli powder and salt to taste. Fold into the salad and transfer to a large serving bowl.

Garnish with mint sprigs if using, and lemon slices. Serve immediately.
Serves 4 to 6

MANGE TOUT SALAD

500 g (1 lb) mange
　tout, trimmed
salt
DRESSING:
3 tablespoons olive
　oil
1 tablespoon lemon
　juice
1 tablespoon chopped
　parsley
2 spring onions,
　sliced
salt and pepper
GARNISH:
8 capers
2 hard-boiled eggs,
　chopped

Cook the mange tout in boiling, salted water until they are just tender. Drain them and set aside to cool.

Place the dressing ingredients in a screw-top jar, seasoning to taste with salt and pepper. Cover and shake to mix well.

Place the mange tout in a serving dish, pour on the dressing and toss. Garnish with the capers and arrange the chopped eggs in strips.
Serves 4

SPICY CHICK PEA SALAD

250 g (8 oz) chick
　peas, soaked
　overnight
salt
4 tablespoons Ginger
　dressing (see box
　tip page 100)
1 green pepper,
　cored, deseeded and
　diced
1 red pepper, cored,
　deseeded and diced
2 tablespoons
　chopped parsley

Drain the chick peas, place in a pan and cover with cold water. Bring to the boil. Boil for 10 minutes then simmer for 1½ to 2 hours or until softened, adding a little salt towards the end of cooking.

Drain thoroughly and place in a bowl. Pour over the dressing and toss well while still warm. Leave to cool.

Add the remaining ingredients, toss thoroughly and transfer to a serving dish.
Serves 6

ORANGE AND PASTA SALAD

500 g (1 lb) fresh
  tagliatelle
4 heads of chicory,
  sliced
6 large oranges,
  segmented
2 tablespoons
  chopped tarragon
4 tablespoons snipped
  chives
DRESSING:
6 tablespoons olive
  oil
2 tablespoons each
  orange and lemon
  juice
1/2 teaspoon coarse-
  grain mustard
1 teaspoon each clear
  honey, mixed
  herbs and finely
  grated orange rind

Cut the tagliatelle into shorter lengths and cook until *al dente*. Drain and cool quickly under cold running water. Drain thoroughly and place in a large bowl.

Mix the dressing ingredients together and pour over the pasta.

Stir in the chicory, orange segments and herbs. Transfer to a serving dish and serve immediately.

Serves 4 to 6

BROAD BEAN SALAD

500 g (1 lb) shelled
  broad beans
salt
500 g (1 lb) dried
  conchiglie
175 g (6 oz) salami,
  diced
DRESSING:
6 tablespoons
  mayonnaise
2 eggs, hard-boiled
  and diced
2 tablespoons lime
  juice
2 teaspoons finely
  grated lime rind
4 tablespoons snipped
  chives
2 tablespoons
  chopped thyme
TO GARNISH:
thyme sprig

Cook the broad beans in boiling salted water for 5 minutes. Drain and set aside.

Cook the pasta according to the packet instructions. Drain and cool quickly under cold running water. Drain thoroughly and place in a large bowl. Stir in the beans and salami.

Mix the dressing ingredients together and fold into the pasta and beans. Spoon the salad into a serving bowl and garnish with a sprig of thyme.

Serves 4 to 6

SPINACH OMELETTE WEDGES

375 g (12 oz)
  spinach
15 g (½ oz) butter
2 tablespoons olive
  oil
1 onion, chopped
6 eggs
50 g (2 oz)
  Dolcelatte or other
  blue-veined cheese,
  diced
salt and pepper

Cook the spinach with just the water clinging to its leaves after washing, for 6 to 8 minutes. Drain well, squeeze dry, then chop finely.

Heat the butter and 1 tablespoon of oil in a pan, add the onion and fry until softened. Mix with the spinach.

Break the eggs into a bowl, add the cheese, spinach mixture and seasoning.

Heat the remaining oil in a 23 cm (9 inch) frying pan, add the egg mixture and stir lightly until beginning to set. Cook for about 5 minutes, until the underneath is set, then invert a large plate over the pan, turn the pan over and ease the omelette onto the plate. Add a little more oil to the pan, heat it then slide the omelette back into the pan and cook until the other side is set.

Cut into wedges and serve with salad and wholewheat bread.
Serves 4

RADICCHIO SALAD

2 heads of radicchio
4 tablespoons olive
  oil
1 tablespoon red wine
  vinegar
3 cloves garlic, finely
  chopped
1 tablespoon grated
  Parmesan cheese
1 tablespoon chopped
  basil
salt and pepper

Remove the outer leaves from the radicchio and cut away the thick stems. Separate the leaves, tearing any larger leaves into smaller bite-sized pieces. Wash, dry thoroughly then place in a serving bowl.

To make the dressing, beat the oil with the vinegar, garlic, Parmesan, basil and salt and pepper to taste. Pour over the radicchio and toss lightly to mix. Serve as an accompaniment to pasta dishes or grilled meats like lamb.
Serve 4 to 6

BEAN AND PEPPERONI SALAD

432 g (15 oz) can red
  kidney beans,
  drained
432 g (15 oz) can
  cannellini beans,
  drained
275 g (9 oz)
  pepperoni or garlic
  sausage, thickly
  sliced
275 g (9 oz) green
  beans, sliced and
  cooked
3 spring onions,
  thinly sliced
3 oranges
1 tablespoon clear
  honey
1 tablespoon French
  mustard
4-5 tablespoons olive
  oil
2 tablespoons lemon
  juice
1 clove garlic, crushed
salt and pepper

Mix the canned beans with the pepperoni, green beans and spring onions in a large bowl. Remove all the skin and pith from two of the oranges and segment. Add to the salad mixture, mixing well.

Squeeze the juice from the remaining orange. Whisk in the honey, mustard, oil, lemon juice, garlic and salt and pepper to taste. Pour over the bean salad mixture and toss well to coat. Serve lightly chilled.
Serves 6

ITALIAN SIMMERED VEGETABLES

75 g (3 oz) butter
3 tablespoons oil
3 onions, sliced
1 clove garlic, crushed
2 large red peppers, cored, seeded and sliced
1 large yellow pepper, cored, seeded and sliced
1 large courgette, sliced
1 stick celery, sliced
325 g (11 oz) canned tomatoes, chopped
4 tablespoons white wine vinegar
1 teaspoon chopped fresh basil
salt and pepper

Heat the butter and oil in a large pan. Add the onions and garlic and cook until softened, about 5 minutes. Add the peppers, courgette, celery, tomatoes, vinegar, basil and salt and pepper to taste, mixing well. Cover and simmer very gently for about 40 minutes, until cooked and tender, stirring occasionally.

Serve piping hot, dusted with Parmesan cheese if liked.

Serves 4

ADRIATIC SEAFOOD SALAD

20 fresh mussels, scrubbed and cleaned
4 scallops
250 g (8 oz) smoked haddock
150 ml (¼ pint) dry vermouth
150 ml (¼ pint) fish stock
1 bouquet garni
salt and pepper
1 × 170 g (6 oz) can crab meat, flaked
125 g (4 oz) cooked peeled prawns
DRESSING:
50 ml (2 fl oz) mayonnaise
50 g (2 oz) thick set natural yogurt
2 eggs, hard-boiled
1 tablespoon capers
½ cucumber, diced
TO SERVE:
2 small lettuce

Put the mussels, scallops and haddock in a shallow pan and pour over the vermouth and stock. Add the bouquet garni and salt and pepper to taste. Bring to the boil and cook for 4 minutes, until the mussel shells have opened and the haddock is tender. Carefully remove from the stock with a slotted spoon, discarding any mussels that have not opened. Remove the shells. Place all the cooked fish in a bowl and allow to cool then add the crab meat and prawns, mixing well.

To make the dressing, mix the mayonnaise with the yogurt, chopped hard-boiled egg, capers, cucumber and salt and pepper to taste. Add to the fish mixture and mix gently.

To serve, arrange the lettuce in individual serving dishes then spoon the prepared seafood salad on top. Serve lightly chilled.

Serve 4 to 6

LEFT: *Radicchio Salad*

RIGHT: *Adriatic Seafood Salad*

AUBERGINE AND TOMATO PIE

750 g (1½ lb)
  aubergines
salt and pepper
flour for dusting
6 tablespoons
  olive oil
  (approximately)
300 ml (½ pint)
  Speedy Tomato
  Sauce (see page
  155)
125 g (4 oz)
  Mozzarella or Bel
  Paese cheese,
  thinly sliced
3 tablespoons grated
  Parmesan cheese

Cut the aubergines lengthways into 5 mm (¼ inch) slices. Sprinkle with salt, place in a colander, cover and leave for 1 hour. Pat dry with kitchen paper, then dust with flour.

Heat half the oil in a large frying pan, add half the aubergine slices and fry briskly until lightly browned on both sides. Remove with a slotted spoon and drain on kitchen paper. Repeat with the remaining oil and aubergine.

Fill an oiled 1.2 litre (2 pint) pie dish with alternate layers of tomato sauce, aubergine, Mozzarella or Bel Paese and a sprinkling of pepper and Parmesan, finishing with Parmesan.

Bake in a preheated moderately hot oven, 200°C (400°F), Gas Mark 6, for 25 to 30 minutes until golden.
Serves 4

STUFFED MUSHROOMS

12 large open-cup
  mushrooms
5-6 tablespoons olive
  oil
1 large onion,
  chopped
1 clove garlic, crushed
40 g (1½ oz) fresh
  breadcrumbs
50 g (2 oz) cooked
  ham or bacon,
  chopped
2 tablespoons
  chopped parsley
2 tablespoons grated
  Parmesan cheese
salt and pepper
parsley sprigs to
  garnish

Remove the stalks from the mushrooms and chop them finely. Heat 3 tablespoons of the oil in a pan, add the onion, garlic and chopped mushroom stalks and fry gently for 5 minutes. Add the breadcrumbs and fry until crisp, then stir in the ham or bacon, parsley, cheese, and salt and pepper to taste.

Arrange the mushroom caps, hollow side up, in a well oiled shallow ovenproof dish. Fill with the stuffing and sprinkle with a little oil.

Cover loosely with foil. Cook in a preheated moderately hot oven, 190°C (375°F), Gas Mark 5, for 25 minutes.

Serve hot, garnished with parsley, as a starter, or with chicken, meat or fish.
Serves 4

POTATO GNOCCHI

175 g (6 oz) plain
  flour
1 egg, beaten
salt and pepper
grated nutmeg
500 g (1 lb) potatoes,
  boiled and mashed
TO SERVE:
25 g (1 oz) butter
25 g (1 oz) grated
  Parmesan cheese
Chicken Liver Sauce
  or Meat Sauce (see
  page 154)

Combine the flour, egg, and salt, pepper and nutmeg to taste with the potato. Mix well to form a firm dough. With floured hands, shape pieces of the dough into long rolls, about 1 cm (½ inch) thick. Cut into 2 cm (¾ inch) lengths and curve by denting with a little finger.

Cook in batches, by dropping into a large pan of boiling salted water and simmering for 3 to 5 minutes until they rise to the surface. Lift out with a slotted spoon and drain. Place in a buttered shallow dish, dot with butter and sprinkle with Parmesan.

Place in a preheated moderately hot oven, 200°C (400°F), Gas Mark 6, for 7 to 10 minutes.

Divide between individual dishes and pour over the sauce.
Serves 4

PEPPERS WITH TOMATOES

4 tablespoons oil
250 g (8 oz) onions,
   chopped
2 cloves garlic,
   crushed
2 bay leaves
6 large green peppers,
   halved, cored and
   deseeded
500 g (1 lb)
   tomatoes, skinned
   and chopped
salt and pepper

Heat the oil in a wide pan, add the onions, garlic and bay leaves and fry gently for 5 minutes, stirring occasionally.

Cut the peppers into 1 cm (½ inch) strips and add to the pan. Stir lightly, then cover and cook gently for 10 minutes.

Add the tomatoes and a little salt and pepper and cook uncovered, stirring frequently, until most of the liquid has evaporated and the mixture is fairly thick. Remove the bay leaves and check the seasoning.

Serve hot with grilled chicken, chops or steaks, or cold as an antipasto.

Serves 4

SPINACH PUDDING

50 g (2 oz) butter
1 onion, grated
500 g (1 lb) chopped
   frozen spinach,
   thawed
25 g (1 oz) plain
   flour
200 ml (7 fl oz) milk
25 g (1 oz) grated
   Parmesan cheese
3 eggs, separated
salt and pepper
grated nutmeg
300 ml (½ pint)
   Speedy Tomato
   Sauce (see page
   155)

Melt half the butter in a saucepan, add the onion and fry gently for 5 minutes. Stir in the spinach, cover and cook for 5 minutes. Uncover and cook, stirring, until the moisture has evaporated.

Melt the remaining butter in a clean pan, add the flour and cook, stirring, until browned. Add the milk and cook, stirring, for 2 minutes until thick and smooth. Remove from the heat and beat in the cheese, egg yolks, spinach, and salt, pepper and nutmeg to taste.

Whisk the egg whites until stiff and fold into the mixture. Turn into a well buttered 1.5 litre (2½ pint) pudding basin and cover with buttered foil. Place in a roasting tin half-filled with boiling water. Cook in a preheated moderate oven, 180°C (350°F), Gas Mark 4, for about 1 hour, until firm in the centre.

Leave for 5 minutes, then turn out and pour over the sauce to serve.

Serves 4

MEDITERRANEAN VEGETABLES

1 small aubergine
salt and pepper
1½ tablespoons oil
1 small onion, sliced
1 small clove garlic,
   crushed
1 celery stick,
   chopped
½ green pepper,
   cored, deseeded and
   chopped
2 tomatoes, skinned
   and chopped
2 tablespoons water
½ teaspoon dried
   oregano
½ teaspoon dried
   basil
chopped parsley to
   garnish

Cut the aubergine into thin slices and sprinkle with salt. Place in a colander and leave for 30 minutes. Rinse and pat dry with kitchen paper.

Heat the oil in a saucepan and add the aubergine, onion, garlic, celery and green pepper. Cook, stirring, until all the vegetables are coated with oil. Cover and cook for 10 minutes. Add the tomatoes, water, oregano, basil and salt and pepper to taste. Bring to the boil, cover and simmer for 30 minutes.

Serve hot or cold, sprinkled with parsley.

Serves 2

PIZZAS

Pizza, so the legend goes, is said to have been invented by the resourceful bakers in the back streets of Naples as a way of making a little food stretch a long way. However, there are almost as many tales on the origins of pizza as there are of the origins of pasta, some dating back to the Roman times. Whatever the origins, today there are endless recipes and variations for this very popular dish.

Some say the secrets of a good pizza lie in the dough used, how it is rolled out and how it is cooked; other talk more about the topping, skilfully mixing and matching ingredients liked cured meats and sausages, cheese, herbs, anchovies, vegetables and tomatoes for success; yet most agree the specially brick-built pizza ovens, found all over Italy, bring a truly authentic baked crispiness and aroma to the best-loved pizzas.

Even-so, home-made pizzas can capture some of those finer qualities and they are easy and fun to make. They also cross the age gap barrier with food since they are appreciated equally by adults and children alike – making splendid party food.

BABY PIZZAS

1 quantity pizza
   dough (see
   below
1 quantity tomato
   sauce (see below)
TOPPING:
125 g (4 oz)
   Mozzarella
   cheese, diced
1 tablespoon grated
   Parmesan cheese
125 g (4 oz) Italian
   Mortadella or
   salami, chopped
1-2 cloves garlic,
   crushed

Prepare the pizza dough and tomato sauce as for Pizza Napoletana (below). When the dough has risen, knead it again and divide into 8 or 12 pieces. Form each into a round.

Heat a little oil in a large frying pan and fry 2 or 3 rounds at a time for about 5 to 7 minutes, until golden brown on each side.

Spread the hot sauce on the pizzas and top with the cheeses, Mortadella or salami and garlic. Return to the pan and cook for 3 minutes. Fold in half and serve immediately.
Serves 4 to 6

PIZZA NAPOLETANA

PIZZA DOUGH:
300 g (10 oz) strong
   white plain flour
pinch of salt
1 teaspoon dried yeast
1 teaspoon caster
   sugar
250 ml (8 fl oz)
   warm water
   (approx)
TOMATO SAUCE:
1 tablespoon oil
1 onion, chopped
1 clove garlic, crushed
1 × 397 g (14 oz)
   can chopped
   tomatoes
2 tablespoons dry
   white wine
½ teaspoon each
   dried oregano and
   basil
salt and pepper
1 tablespoon tomato
   purée
TOPPING:
125 g (4 oz)
   Mozzarella or
   Cheddar cheese,
   diced
1 tablespoon capers
   (optional)

Sift the flour and salt into a bowl. Mix the yeast with the sugar and 2 tablespoons of the water and leave for 10 minutes, then add to the flour with enough water to give a firm dough. Knead on a floured surface for about 15 minutes, until the dough is elastic. Cover with a cloth and leave in a warm place until doubled in size.

Press the dough into the base and sides of a 23 cm (9 inch) loose-bottomed tin or flan ring placed on a baking sheet.

Heat the oil in a pan, add the onion and garlic and cook for 2 to 3 minutes, until translucent. Add the tomatoes with their juice, the wine, herbs, and salt and pepper to taste. Bring to the boil and cook rapidly for 12 to 15 minutes, until thickened. Stir in the tomato purée.

Spread evenly over the dough and arrange the cheese and capers, if using, on top. Bake in a preheated hot oven, 220°C (425°F), Gas Mark 7, for 20 minutes, until golden brown.

Serve hot.
Serves 6 to 8

QUICK PIZZAS

4 slices bread
15 g (½ oz) butter or
    margarine
75 g (3 oz) Edam
    cheese, grated
2 tomatoes, sliced
1 teaspoon mixed
    herbs
salt and pepper
50 g (2 oz) lean
    ham, cut into strips
TO GARNISH:
parsley sprigs
tomato wedges

Toast the bread lightly on both sides and cover with the butter or margarine.

Arrange half the cheese on the toast then top with the tomato slices. Sprinkle with the mixed herbs and salt and pepper to taste. Top with the remaining cheese, then arrange the ham in a lattice pattern over the top.

Place under a preheated moderate grill until the cheese has melted. Serve immediately, garnished with parsley and tomato wedges.
Serves 4

MUSHROOM AND MOZZARELLA PIZZA

1 quantity Pizza
    Dough (see page
    151)
8 tablespoons passata
125 g (4 oz) mixed
    mushrooms, sliced
125 g (4 oz)
    Mozzarella
    cheese, sliced
2 tablespoons olive
    oil
½ teaspoon dried
    oregano
salt and pepper

Roll out the pizza dough (see page 151) and spread with the passata to within 2.5 cm (1 inch) of the edges.

Top with the mushrooms and Mozzarella cheese. Sprinkle over the olive oil, oregano and salt and pepper to taste.

Slide the pizza onto a hot baking sheet and bake at once, in a preheated hot oven, 220°C (425°F), Gas Mark 7, for 15 to 20 minutes, until golden, cooked through and the cheese has melted. Serve immediately.
Serves 4

LEFT: *Baby Pizzas; Pizza Napoletana*

RIGHT: *Pan Pizza*

PAN PIZZA

½ teaspoon dried
    yeast
½ teaspoon sugar
75 g (3 oz) strong
    white plain flour
75 g (3 oz)
    wholemeal flour
pinch of salt
50 g (2 oz) butter
1 egg, beaten
little milk to mix
FILLING:
65 g (2½ oz) tomato
    purée
250 g (8 oz)
    tomatoes, sliced
1 clove garlic, sliced
½ teaspoon each dried
    oregano and basil
75 g (3 oz)
    Mozzarella, cubed
1 × 340 g (12 oz)
    can asparagus,
    drained
125 g (4 oz) mushrooms
few stuffed olives

Dissolve the yeast and sugar in a little warm water. Place the flours and salt in a bowl and rub in the butter until the mixture resembles fine breadcrumbs. Mix in the egg, dissolved yeast and a little milk to give a firm dough. Knead for 5 to 10 minutes, until smooth and elastic. Place in a bowl, cover with a cloth and leave to rise in a warm place for 1½ hours, until doubled in size.

Lightly grease a large heavy-based frying pan. Knead the dough again and roll out on a floured surface to the pan size. Place in the pan and bring a little dough up the sides.

Spread the tomato purée over the base, arrange the tomatoes on top and sprinkle with the garlic, herbs and cheese. Arrange the asparagus, mushrooms and olives on top.

Cook over a medium heat for 15 to 20 minutes, then place under a preheated hot grill for 1 to 2 minutes, until the cheese is golden. Serve hot.
Serves 4 to 6

HOME-STYLE PIZZA

PIZZA DOUGH:
15 g (½ oz) fresh
   yeast
2 tablespoons warm
   water
250 g (8 oz) plain
   flour
1 teaspoon salt
2 tablespoons olive
   oil
3 tablespoons milk
TOPPING:
3 tablespoons olive
   oil
500 g (1 lb)
   tomatoes, skinned,
   deseeded and
   chopped
1 teaspoon dried
   oregano or basil
salt and pepper
175 g (6 oz)
   Mozzarella
   cheese, sliced
4 tablespoons grated
   Parmesan cheese
6-8 black olives

Cream the yeast with the water. Sift the flour and salt into a bowl, make a well in the centre and pour in the yeast, oil and milk. Mix to a firm but pliable dough, adding a little more milk if necessary.

Turn onto a floured surface and knead vigorously for 5 minutes. Place in a clean basin, cover and leave to rise in a warm place until doubled in size.

Knead the dough lightly, then cut in half. Roll each piece into a 20 to 23 cm (8 to 9 inch) circle.

Place the circles on oiled baking sheets and brush with some of the oil. Cover with tomatoes and sprinkle with the herbs, and salt and pepper to taste. Add the cheese slices, then top with the Parmesan and olives.

Spoon over the remaining oil and leave to rise in a warm place for 30 minutes.

Bake in a preheated hot oven, 220°C (425°F), Gas Mark 7, for 25 to 30 minutes. Serve immediately.
Serves 4

INDIVIDUAL PIZZAS

1 quantity risen
   Pizza dough (see
   Home-Style
   Pizza, left)
TOPPING:
3 tablespoons olive
   oil
500 g (1 lb) tomatoes,
   skinned, deseeded
   and chopped
salt and pepper
TO FINISH:
125 g (4 oz)
   mushrooms, sliced
   and fried
2-3 garlic cloves,
   finely chopped
2-3 tablespoons
   grated Parmesan

Divide the risen dough into 6 portions, shape into balls and roll into 10 cm (4 inch) circles.

Brush with half of the oil, cover with the tomatoes and season well.

Top with the mushrooms, garlic and cheese. Sprinkle with the remaining oil and leave to rise in a warm place for about 15 minutes.

Bake in a preheated hot oven, 220°C (425°F), Gas Mark 7, for about 15 minutes. Serve immediately.
Serves 6
ALTERNATIVE FINISHES:
1. Chopped salami and olives.
2. Sliced peppers, diced Mozzarella cheese and strips of anchovy fillet.

SAN REMO PIZZA

1 quantity risen
   Pizza dough (see
   Home-Style Pizza,
   left)
TOPPING:
7 tablespoons olive
   oil
625 g (1¼ lb)
   onions, finely
   sliced
1-2 cloves garlic,
   crushed
1 × 397 g (14 oz)
   can chopped
   tomatoes, drained
1 teaspoon dried
   oregano
salt and pepper
1 × 50 g (2 oz) can
   anchovy fillets, cut
   in strips
20 black olives

To make the topping, heat 4 tablespoons of the oil in a saucepan, add the onions and fry gently until soft and golden. Add the garlic, tomatoes, oregano, and a little salt and pepper. Cook, uncovered, until reduced and thickened. Check the seasoning and leave to cool.

Turn the risen dough onto a floured surface and knead lightly. Cut in half, shape each into a ball and place in well oiled 20 to 23 cm (8 to 9 inch) pie plates. Press out the dough to cover the base of the plates and reach 1 cm (½ inch) up the sides. Brush with 1 tablespoon oil.

Spread the tomato mixture over the dough and arrange the anchovy strips and olives on top. Sprinkle over the remaining oil.

Bake in a preheated hot oven, 220°C (425°F), Gas Mark 7, for 25 to 30 minutes. Serve immediately.
Serves 4 to 6

San Remo Pizza; Individual Pizzas; Home-Style Pizza

MUSHROOM AND PEPPER PIZZAS

PIZZA BASE:
150 ml (¼ pint) milk
125 g (4 oz) butter
25 g (1 oz) fresh yeast
3 eggs, beaten
500 g (1 lb) plain flour
1 teaspoon salt

PIZZA TOPPING:
2 tablespoons oil
2 large onions, chopped
2 × 397 g (14 oz) cans chopped tomatoes
2 cloves garlic, crushed
1 small bay leaf
1 teaspoon dried basil
1 teaspoon dried oregano
salt and pepper

TO FINISH:
125 g (4 oz) mushrooms, sliced and fried in butter
1 green pepper, sliced

Put the milk and butter in a small pan and heat gently until warm. Remove from the heat, add the yeast and blend well, then beat in the eggs.

Sift the flour and salt into a large bowl, add the yeast liquid and mix to a soft dough. Cover and leave to rise in a warm place for about 45 minutes.

Meanwhile, make the topping. Heat the oil in a frying pan, add the onions and cook gently until soft. Add the tomatoes with their juice, garlic, herbs and salt and pepper to taste and bring to the boil. Cook for about 20 minutes, stirring occasionally, until the sauce is thick. Cool.

Turn the dough onto a floured surface and cut into 4 pieces. Roll each piece out to a 20 cm (8 inch) circle and place on a greased baking sheet. Stand a 20 cm (8 inch) flan ring round each one.

Divide the topping between the pizzas, and arrange the mushrooms and pepper slices on top. Cover and leave in a warm place for about 10 minutes.

Bake in a preheated hot oven, 230°C (450°F), Gas Mark 8, for 35-40 minutes.
Makes 4

Mushroom and Pepper Pizzas; Ham Pizzas; Anchovy Pizzas

HAM PIZZAS

4 pizza bases (see above)
1 recipe pizza topping (see above)

TO FINISH:
125 g (4 oz) cooked ham, chopped
50 g (2 oz) large black olives

Place the pizzas on baking sheets and surround with flan rings, (see above). Mix the ham and olives into the topping and spoon over the pizzas.

Rise, bake and serve as above.
Makes 4

ANCHOVY PIZZAS

4 pizza bases (see above)
1 recipe pizza topping (see above)

TO FINISH:
250 g (8 oz) Cheddar cheese, sliced
2 × 50 g (2 oz) cans anchovy fillets

Place the pizzas on baking sheets and surround with flan rings (see above). Spoon the topping over the pizzas, cover with cheese and arrange the anchovies on top.

Rise, bake and serve as above.
Makes 4

SMOKED SALMON AND DILL PIZZA

1 quantity Pizza
    Dough (see page
    151)
3 Provence or extra-
    large tomatoes,
    skinned and sliced
175 g (6 oz) smoked
    salmon, thinly
    sliced
1 tablespoon each
    chopped dill and
    parsley
125 g (4 oz)
    Mozzarella
    cheese, sliced

Roll out the dough (see page 151). Arrange the tomatoes on the base and lay the salmon on top. Sprinkle with the herbs and cover with the cheese.

Slide the pizza onto a hot baking sheet (see page 151) and bake at once in a preheated hot oven, 220°C (425°F), Gas Mark 7, for 15 to 20 minutes, until golden. Serve immediately.

Serves 4

NOTE: For a less expensive variation, use peeled prawns instead of salmon.

BACON AND MUSHROOM PIZZAS

4 pizza bases (see
    Italian Pizzas
    page 120)
2 × 400 g (14 oz)
    cans peeled
    tomatoes
2 teaspoons grated
    onion
250 g (8 oz) matured
    Cheddar cheese,
    grated
6 rashers streaky
    bacon, derinded
50 g (2 oz)
    mushrooms, sliced
oil for brushing

Place the prepared pizza bases on oiled baking sheets. Drain and chop the tomatoes, then spread over the bases.

Sprinkle the onion and 175 g (6 oz) of the cheese over the tomatoes. Stretch the bacon and cut into strips. Arrange in a lattice pattern over the cheese and place the mushrooms in the squares, brushing them with a little oil. Sprinkle with the remaining cheese. Bake as for Italian pizzas (page 120). Serve immediately.

Makes 4

ROMAN PIZZA

1 quantity Pizza
  Dough (see page
  151)
4 Provence or extra-
  large tomatoes,
  skinned and sliced
6 basil leaves, finely
  chopped
1 tablespoon chopped
  oregano
salt and pepper
125 g (4 oz) Parma
  ham, thinly sliced
50 g (2 oz) button
  mushrooms
75 g (3 oz) matured
  Cheddar cheese,
  grated

Roll out the dough (see page 151). Arrange the tomatoes on the base, sprinkle with the herbs, and season with salt and pepper to taste. Lay the Parma ham on top and sprinkle with the mushrooms and cheese.

Slide the pizza onto a hot baking sheet (see page 151) and bake at once in a preheated hot oven, 220°C (425°F), Gas Mark 7, for 15 to 20 minutes, until golden. Serve immediately.
Serves 4

ARTICHOKE AND MUSHROOM PIZZA

1 quantity Pizza
  Dough (see page
  151)
2 tablespoons tomato
  purée
4-6 tomatoes, sliced
2 tablespoons each
  chopped basil and
  oregano
1 × 400 g (14 oz)
  can artichoke
  hearts, drained and
  sliced
50 g (2 oz) button
  mushrooms, sliced
3 tablespoons oil
25 g (1 oz) each
  Parmesan and
  matured Cheddar
  cheese, grated

Roll out the dough (see page 151). Spread the tomato purée thinly over the base. Arrange the tomatoes on top and sprinkle with the herbs. Place the artichokes and mushrooms on top and drizzle over the oil. Sprinkle with the cheeses.

Slide the pizza onto a hot baking sheet (see page 151) and bake at once in a preheated hot oven, 220°C (425°F), Gas Mark 7, for 15 to 20 minutes, until golden. Serve immediately.
Serves 4

LEFT: *Smoked Salmon and Dill Pizza; Bacon and Mushroom Pizzas*

RIGHT: *Artichoke and Mushroom Pizza*

GARLIC AND PEPPER PIZZAS

4 pizza bases
  (see Italian Pizzas
  page 120)
2 × 400 g (14 oz)
  cans tomatoes,
  drained and
  chopped
1 tablespoon oil
1 onion, chopped
1 green pepper,
  cored, deseeded and
  chopped
125 g (4 oz)
  Emmental cheese,
  sliced
125 g (4 oz) garlic
  sausage, sliced
1 tablespoon chopped
  mixed herbs
50 g (2 oz) Parmesan
  cheese, grated

Place the prepared pizzas on oiled baking sheets and cover with the tomatoes.

Heat the oil in a pan, add the onion and green pepper and fry until soft. Spoon over the tomatoes. Cover with the sliced cheese then the garlic sausage. Sprinkle with the herbs and Parmesan cheese. Bake as for Italian Pizzas (page 120). Serve immediately.
Makes 4

FRYPAN PIZZA

Frypan Pizza

1 × 102 g (4 oz)
  packet instant
  potato
1 tablespoon dried
  onion
450 ml (¾ pint)
  boiling water
2 eggs
2 tablespoons plain
  flour
15 g (½ oz) butter
1 tablespoon oil
1 × 250 g (8 oz) jar
  tomato and herb
  pizza topping
2 cloves garlic,
  chopped
3 tomatoes, cut into
  thin segments
50 g (2 oz) peperami
1 tablespoon capers
salt and pepper
50 g (2 oz) matured
  Cheddar cheese
½ teaspoon dried
  oregano
TO GARNISH:
black olives
thin onion rings
parsley sprig

Put the potato powder and onion into a basin. Pour on the boiling water and stir with a fork. Quickly stir in one egg at a time and then the flour to make a thick, smooth mixture.

Melt the butter and oil in a 23 cm (9 inch) heavy-based frying pan, add the potato mixture and smooth to make an even layer. Cook over a low heat for 5 minutes, then place under a preheated hot grill, 5 to 8 cm (2 to 3 inches) from heat, for 5 minutes or until the top begins to brown.

Quickly spread with the pizza topping and sprinkle with the garlic. Arrange the tomato in a circle around the edge. Cut the peperami in half crossways then lengthways and arrange like the spokes of a wheel. Sprinkle with the capers, and salt and pepper to taste.

Slice the cheese thinly and place between the peperami. Sprinkle with the oregano. Return to the grill until the cheese is bubbling.

Garnish with olives, onions and parsley and serve immediately, with a green salad.

Serves 4 to 6

ITALIAN PIZZAS

BASE:
½ × 567 g (20 oz)
  packet white bread
  mix
200 ml (7 fl oz)
  water
2 teaspoons oil
TOPPING:
2 × 400 g (14 oz)
  cans tomatoes,
  drained
2 teaspoons dried
  oregano
175 g (6 oz)
  Mozzarella or
  Gruyère cheese,
  sliced
salt and pepper
125 g (4 oz)
  pepperoni or spicy
  sausage, sliced
1 small onion, sliced
  into rings
50 g (2 oz) Parmesan
  cheese, grated

Make up the bread mix with the water as directed on the packet. Turn onto a floured surface and knead for 2 minutes. Place in a bowl, cover and leave to rise in a warm place for 20 to 30 minutes, or until the dough has doubled in size.

Turn onto a floured surface and knead for 5 minutes. Divide into 4 pieces and roll out each to a 15 cm (6 inch) circle. Brush with a little oil and place on oiled baking sheets.

Arrange the tomatoes over the pizzas. Top with the oregano, Mozzarella or Gruyère, and salt and pepper to taste. Top with the pepperoni slices and onion rings and sprinkle with the Parmesan cheese.

Bake in a preheated moderately hot oven, 200°C (400°F), Gas Mark 6, for 20 to 25 minutes until the cheese is bubbling. Serve immediately.

Makes 4

PARTY PIZZA

1½ quantity Pizza
  Dough (see page
  151)
1½ quantity Tomato
  Sauce (see Spicy
  Hot Pizza, page
  122)
125 g (4 oz) button
  mushrooms, sliced
8 canned artichoke
  hearts, sliced
6 tomatoes, sliced
6 oregano sprigs
1 × 198 g (7 oz) can
  tuna fish, drained
2 tablespoons capers
2 × 50 g (2 oz) cans
  anchovies, drained
  and mashed
50 g (2 oz) green
  olives, chopped
125 g (4 oz) salami
50 g (2 oz)
  Mozzarella
  cheese, diced
125 g (4 oz) ham
50 g (2 oz) sweetcorn
2 teaspoons dried
  mixed herbs
2 tablespoons olive
  oil
75 g (3 oz) matured
  Cheddar cheese,
  grated

Roll out the dough to fit a large baking sheet, measuring 25 × 30 cm (10 × 12 inches); turn during rolling to prevent shrinking.

Place on a large piece of floured cardboard (see page 151). Using fingertips, push the dough out from the centre to make the edges twice as thick as the rest.

Spread with the tomato sauce. Using a palette knife, lightly divide the dough into 6 sections.

Arrange the mushrooms and artichokes in one section; the tomatoes and oregano in another; the flaked tuna and capers in the third; the mashed anchovies and olives in the fourth; the sliced salami and Mozzarella cheese in the fifth; and the sliced ham and sweetcorn in the last section.

Sprinkle the whole pizza with the mixed herbs, oil and grated cheese.

Slide the pizza onto the hot baking sheet (see page 151) and bake in a preheated hot oven, 230°C (450°F), Gas Mark 8, for 15 to 20 minutes. Cut into slices and serve immediately.
Serves 10

QUICK HAM PIZZA

DOUGH:
125 g (4 oz) self-
  raising flour
½ teaspoon baking
  powder
½ teaspoon made
  mustard
¼ teaspoon salt
25 g (1 oz) Cheddar
  cheese, grated
½ teaspoon paprika
25 g (1 oz) butter
1 egg, beaten
1 tablespoon milk
TOPPING:
50 g (2 oz) butter
1 large onion,
  chopped
1 small green pepper,
  cored, deseeded and
  chopped
175 g (6 oz) ham
50 g (2 oz) garlic
  sausage

Mix together all the dough ingredients then knead lightly on a floured board. Roll out to a 23 cm (9 inch) round and place on a well greased baking sheet. Either fold up the edges of the dough to make a rim, or put a flan ring around the outside of the pizza. Chill while preparing the topping.

Melt the butter in a frying pan, add the onion and pepper and fry until the onion begins to brown. Cut the ham and garlic sausage into thin strips and mix with the onion and pepper. Spread over the pizza base. Bake in a preheated moderately hot oven, 200°C (400°F), Gas Mark 6, for 30 minutes. Serve immediately.
Makes one 23 cm (9 inch) pizza

Party Pizza

'TURNED-OVER' PIZZAS

1 quantity Pizza
Dough (see page
151)
oil for frying
1 quantity Tomato
Sauce (see Spicy
Hot Pizza,
opposite)
125 g (4 oz) matured
Cheddar cheese,
diced
2 tablespoons grated
Parmesan cheese
125 g (4 oz) Italian
salami, sliced
1 tablespoon each
chopped oregano
and basil
1-2 cloves garlic,
crushed

When the pizza dough has risen, divide it into 4 equal pieces and form each into a round.

Heat a little oil in a large heavy-based frying pan and fry 2 rounds at a time for about 2 to 3 minutes on each side, until golden.

Spread the hot Tomato Sauce on the pizzas, and top with the cheeses, salami, herbs and garlic. Return to the pan and cook at a lower heat for 3 minutes. Fold in half and serve immediately.

Serves 4

SEAFOOD PIZZA

1 quantity Pizza
Dough (see page
151)
1 quantity Tomato
Sauce (see Spicy
Hot Pizza,
opposite)
2 tomatoes, skinned
and sliced
1 × 198 g (7 oz) can
tuna fish
125 g (4 oz) peeled
prawns
squeeze of lemon
juice
2 teaspoons chopped
basil
25 g (1 oz) each
matured Cheddar
and Mozzarella
cheese, diced
TO GARNISH:
lemon slices

Roll out the dough (see page 151) and slide onto a hot baking sheet. Cover with the Tomato Sauce and place the tomatoes around the edge. Drain and flake the tuna fish and arrange on top with the prawns. Squeeze over the lemon juice. Sprinkle with the basil and cheeses.

Bake at once in a preheated hot oven, 220°C (425°F), Gas Mark 7, for 15 to 20 minutes, until golden. Serve immediately, garnished with lemon slices if desired.

Serves 4

SPICY HOT PIZZA

25 g (1 oz) butter
2 onions, sliced
1 quantity Pizza
Dough (see page
151)
2-3 green chillies,
deseeded and sliced
lengthways
1 tablespoon each
chopped thyme and
marjoram
50 g (2 oz)
Mozzarella
cheese, diced
TOMATO SAUCE:
1-2 tablespoons oil
1 clove garlic, crushed
2-3 shallots, chopped
250 g (8 oz)
tomatoes, skinned,
deseeded and
chopped
150 ml (1/4 pint) dry
white wine
1 teaspoon dried
mixed herbs
salt and pepper
TO GARNISH
(optional):
marjoram sprigs

First make the tomato sauce. Heat the oil in a pan, add the garlic and shallots and cook for about 5 minutes, until golden. Add the tomatoes, wine and mixed herbs. Bring to the boil and cook rapidly for 20 minutes, until thickened. Season with salt and pepper to taste and leave to cool.

Melt the butter in a pan, add the onions and cook for 5 minutes until golden. Leave to cool.

Roll out the dough and slide the pizza onto a hot baking sheet (see page 151). Spread the onions on the base and cover with the tomato sauce. Sprinkle with the chillies, thyme, marjoram and cheese.

Bake at once in a preheated hot oven, 220°C (425°F), Gas Mark 7, for 15 to 20 minutes, until the dough and topping are golden. Garnish with marjoram if liked, and serve immediately.

Serves 4

'Turned-Over' Pizzas; Seafood Pizza; Spicy Hot Pizza

BAKED VEGETABLE PIZZA

125 g (4 oz) mange
    tout
50 g (2 oz) green
    beans
50 g (2 oz) baby
    carrots, sliced
salt
4 canned artichoke
    hearts, drained
25 g (1 oz) butter
25 g (1 oz) flour
150 ml (¼ pint)
    milk
2 tablespoons single
    cream
25 g (1 oz) Parmesan
    cheese, grated
50 g (2 oz) matured
    Cheddar cheese,
    grated
pinch of dried mixed
    herbs
2 egg yolks
1 quantity Pizza
    Dough (see page
    151)

Blanch the mange tout, beans and carrots in boiling salted water for 3 minutes. Drain and leave to cool.

Cut the beans and mange tout in half and slice the artichokes. Mix all the vegetables together and set aside.

Melt the butter in a pan, add the flour and cook for 2 minutes, without browning. Gradually add the milk, bring to the boil, stirring, and cook for 2 minutes. Remove from the heat, stir in the cream, Parmesan cheese, half the Cheddar cheese, herbs and egg yolks. Stir in the vegetables.

Roll out the dough (see page 151), making the edge at least twice as thick as the rest and 2.5 cm (1 inch) high.

Spoon the sauce into the centre and sprinkle over the remaining Cheddar cheese.

Slide the pizza onto a hot baking sheet and bake at once in a preheated hot oven, 220°C (425°F), Gas Mark 7, for 15 to 20 minutes, until golden.

Leave for 10 minutes before serving.
Serves 4

TOMATO AND MOZZARELLA PIZZA

500 g (1 lb) ripe
    plum tomatoes, or
    1 × 400 g (14 oz)
    can tomatoes
2 tablespoons olive
    oil
1 teaspoon salt
1 quantity Pizza
    Dough (see page
    151)
175 g (6 oz)
    Mozzarella
    cheese, grated
1 teaspoon dried
    oregano
1 tablespoon grated
    Parmesan cheese

Roughly chop the tomatoes and place, with their juice, in a frying pan. Add the oil and salt, bring to the boil, cover and cook for 2 minutes. Remove the lid and simmer for 15 minutes, stirring occasionally, until thickened.

Turn the mixture into a sieve and discard any liquid that drains through. Rub the tomatoes through the sieve and leave to cool.

Roll out the dough (see page 151). Sprinkle with the Mozzarella cheese, spoon over the tomato sauce, then sprinkle with the oregano and Parmesan.

Slide the pizza onto a hot baking sheet (see page 151) and bake in a preheated hot oven, 230°C (450°F), Gas Mark 8, for 15 to 20 minutes, until golden brown. Serve immediately.
Serves 4

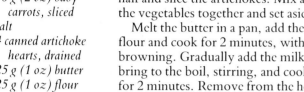

ONION PIZZA

3 tablespoons oil
3 large onions, sliced
    very thinly
2 eggs, beaten
3 tablespoons milk
25 g (1 oz) grated
    Parmesan cheese
salt and pepper
1 quantity Pizza
    Dough (see page
    151)
16 black olives

Heat the oil in a heavy-based pan, add the onions and fry gently for about 10 minutes until softened. Remove from the heat and add the eggs, milk, cheese and salt and pepper to taste.

Roll out the dough and spread with the prepared topping. Garnish with the black olives.

Slide the pizza onto a hot baking sheet (see page 151) and bake at once, in a preheated hot oven, 220°C (425°F), Gas Mark 7, for 15 to 20 minutes, until golden. Serve immediately.
Serves 4

PIZZA PAYSANNE

50 g (2 oz) butter
1 large onion, finely chopped
4 rashers streaky bacon, derinded and chopped
2 potatoes, diced
2 eggs
142 ml (¼ pint) carton double cream
1 tablespoon each chopped parsley, thyme and chives
salt and pepper
1 quantity Pizza Dough (see page 151)
1 small red pepper, cored, deseeded and chopped
125 g (4 oz) matured Cheddar cheese, grated

Melt the butter in a pan, add the onion and bacon and cook for about 5 minutes, until lightly browned. Drain on kitchen paper.

Add the potato to the pan and cook, stirring occasionally, until browned. Drain on kitchen paper.

Beat the eggs and cream together. Stir in the herbs and season liberally with salt and pepper.

When the dough has doubled in size (see page 151), place it on a floured surface and knead thoroughly. Roll out and use to line a 23 cm (9 inch) flan ring placed on a baking sheet.

Spoon the onion, bacon and potato into the case and sprinkle with the red pepper. Pour over the egg mixture and sprinkle with the cheese.

Bake in a preheated moderately hot oven, 200°C (400°F), Gas Mark 6, for 20 to 25 minutes, until well risen and golden. Serve hot or cold.
Serves 4

LEFT: *Baked Vegetable Pizza*

RIGHT: *Tomato and Mozzarella Pizza; Pizza Paysanne*

CHILLI-TOPPED PIZZA

2 tablespoons oil
4 shallots, chopped
½-1 teaspoon chilli
  powder
250 g (8 oz) minced
  beef
1 × 227 g (8 oz) can
  tomatoes
dash of Tabasco sauce
1 × 208 g (7 oz) can
  red kidney beans
1 clove garlic, crushed
salt and pepper
1 quantity Pizza
  Dough (see page
  151)
125 g (4 oz)
  Mozzarella
  cheese, diced
2 teaspoons grated
  Parmesan cheese

Heat the oil in a pan, add the shallots and cook for 2 minutes. Stir in the chilli powder and minced beef and cook until browned, stirring occasionally. Add the tomatoes, with their juice, and Tabasco.

Bring to the boil, cover and simmer for 45 minutes, until very thick, stirring occasionally. Remove from the heat.

Drain and rinse the kidney beans under cold water. Add to the pan with the garlic, and salt and pepper to taste. Leave to cool.

Roll out the dough (see page 151). Slide the pizza onto a hot baking sheet and spoon over the chilli mixture. Sprinkle with the cheeses and bake in a preheated hot oven, 220°C (425°F), Gas Mark 7, for 15 to 20 minutes. Serve immediately.
Serves 4

MEAT AND CHEESE STUFFED PIZZA

4 tablespoons olive
  oil
1 onion, sliced
250 g (8 oz) minced
  beef
125 ml (4 fl oz) dry
  white wine
1-2 cloves garlic,
  crushed
salt and pepper
50 g (2 oz)
  unsmoked ham,
  diced
75 g (3 oz) matured
  Cheddar cheese,
  diced
50 g (2 oz) Ricotta or
  curd cheese
1 quantity Pizza
  Dough (see page
  151)
2 tablespoons fresh
  breadcrumbs,
  toasted

Heat 3 tablespoons of the oil in a pan, add the onion and cook for about 5 minutes, until golden, stirring occasionally. Add the minced beef and cook until browned, stirring constantly.

Add the wine, lower the heat slightly and cook, uncovered, for about 15 minutes, until all the liquid has reduced. Stir in the garlic, and salt and pepper to taste. Transfer to a bowl and leave to cool completely.

Stir the ham and cheeses into the mixture until very smooth.

Knead the dough on a floured surface and divide into 2 unequal pieces. Roll out the larger piece into a 25 to 30 cm (10 to 12 inch) circle and place on a floured piece of circular cardboard (see page 151). Sprinkle with half the breadcrumbs and cover with the filling, leaving a 1 cm (½ inch) border all round. Sprinkle with the remaining breadcrumbs and 1 tablespoon oil.

Roll out the remaining dough to the same size. Dampen the edges with water and place over the stuffing, pinching the edges together to seal well.

Brush the top with a little water and slide the pizza onto a hot baking sheet. Bake in a preheated moderately hot oven, 200°C (400°F), Gas Mark 6, for 25 minutes or until golden.

Leave to stand for 30 to 40 minutes. Cut into wedges to serve.
Serves 4 to 6

Meat and Cheese Stuffed Pizza; Chilli-Topped Pizza

HAM AND CHEESE PIZZA PIE

25 g (1 oz) butter
3 tomatoes, skinned, deseeded and chopped
2 tablespoons dry white wine
6 basil leaves, finely chopped
salt and pepper
2 × quantity Pizza Dough (see page 151)
175 g (6 oz) Mozzarella cheese, sliced
175 g (6 oz) smoked back bacon, derinded and cut into thin strips
50 g (2 oz) matured Cheddar cheese, grated
beaten egg to glaze

Melt the butter in a pan, add the tomatoes and wine, bring to the boil and cook for 5 minutes. Add the basil, and salt and pepper to taste; cool.

When the dough has doubled in size, place it on a floured surface and knead thoroughly. Break off two thirds, roll out into a thin circle and use to line a greased 23 cm (9 inch) loose-bottomed cake tin, ensuring that the dough comes up the side.

Spread the tomato mixture over the base, cover with half the Mozzarella and all the bacon. Lay the remaining cheese slices on top and sprinkle with the Cheddar cheese.

Roll out the remaining dough to fit the top of the pizza, dampen the edges and seal well. Leave in a warm place to rise for 30 to 40 minutes.

Brush with beaten egg and bake in a preheated moderately hot oven, 200°C (400°F), Gas Mark 6, for 15 minutes. Lower the heat to 190°C (375°F), Gas Mark 5, and cook for 20 minutes. Serve immediately.
Serves 6

FOUR SEASONS PIZZA

2 tablespoons oil
1 clove garlic, crushed
125 g (4 oz) button mushrooms, sliced
1 tablespoon parsley
1-2 teaspoons capers
50 g (2 oz) peeled prawns
2 rashers streaky bacon, chopped
2 tablespoons sweetcorn
1 quantity Pizza Dough (see page 151)
½ quantity Tomato Sauce (see Spicy Hot Pizza, page 122)
125 g (4 oz) Mozzarella cheese, diced
2 tomatoes, sliced
4 black olives, halved
1 teaspoon dried mixed herbs

Heat the oil in a pan, add the garlic and mushrooms and cook for 2 minutes. Stir in the parsley and leave to cool.

Mix the capers and prawns together. Mix the bacon and sweetcorn together.

Roll out the dough (see page 151). Spread the Tomato Sauce over the base and sprinkle with the cheese. Using a palette knife, gently mark the pizza into quarters.

Arrange the mushrooms on one quarter, the prawns on another, sprinkle the bacon and sweetcorn on the third quarter, and arrange the tomatoes and olives on the last quarter. Sprinkle the herbs all over.

Slide the pizza onto a hot baking sheet and bake at once in a preheated hot oven, 220°C (425°F), Gas Mark 7, for 15 to 20 minutes, until golden. Serve immediately.
Serves 4

Ham and Cheese Pizza Pie; Four Seasons Pizza

ASPARAGUS AND TOMATO PAN PIZZA

1 × 65 g (2½ oz) can tomato purée
1 clove garlic, crushed
½ teaspoon each dried basil and oregano
1 quantity Pizza Dough (see page 151)
25 g (1 oz) Mozzarella cheese, grated
250 g (8 oz) tomatoes, skinned and sliced
250 g (8 oz) frozen asparagus, thawed
75 g (3 oz) Mozzarella cheese, cubed
1 tablespoon grated Parmesan cheese

Mix together the tomato purée, garlic and herbs.

Lightly grease a very large heavy-based frying pan. Roll out the dough on a floured board to the size of the pan. Place in the pan and bring a little dough up the sides.

Sprinkle over the Mozzarella cheese and spoon the tomato purée mixture on top. Arrange the tomatoes and asparagus over the pizza and sprinkle with the Mozzarella and Parmesan cheese.

Cook over medium heat for 15 to 20 minutes, then place under a preheated hot grill for 1 to 2 minutes until golden. Serve immediately.
Serves 4

PIZZA TURNOVERS

1 quantity Pizza Dough (see page 151)
olive oil for brushing
4 tomatoes, skinned, deseeded and chopped
1 tablespoon chopped basil
6 small slices Mozzarella cheese
175 g (6 oz) peeled prawns
25 g (1 oz) matured Cheddar cheese, grated
salt and pepper
oil for deep-frying

Divide the dough into 6 equal pieces. Roll out each piece very thinly into a 15 cm (6 inch) circle, turning the dough to prevent shrinking. Brush the centre of each circle with a little olive oil and the edge with water.

Divide the tomatoes between the circles, placing in the centre, and sprinkle with the basil. Place a slice of Mozzarella on top, then the prawns. Sprinkle with the grated cheese and season liberally with salt and pepper.

Fold the dough over the filling to form a crescent and seal the edges well. Place on a floured board, cover with a clean tea-towel and leave to rise in a warm place for 25 to 30 minutes.

Heat the oil in a deep pan, add 2 'turnovers' at a time and cook for 5 to 6 minutes on each side, until golden. Drain on kitchen paper and serve immediately.
Serves 6

FRENCH BREAD PIZZA

1 French loaf
2 tablespoons oil
1 × 65 g (2½ oz) can tomato purée
1 teaspoon dried mixed herbs
1-2 cloves garlic, crushed
3 tomatoes, sliced
175 g (6 oz) peeled prawns
125 g (4 oz) Mozzarella cheese, grated
2 teaspoons capers
125 g (4 oz) salami, sliced
8 stuffed olives, sliced
125 g (4 oz) Gruyère cheese, grated

Cut the bread in half lengthways, brush the crust with the oil, and spread the tomato purée over the cut surfaces. Sprinkle with the herbs and garlic.

Arrange the tomatoes, prawns and Mozzarella cheese on one half. Sprinkle with the capers.

Arrange the salami and olives on the other half. Sprinkle with the Gruyère cheese.

Cut each piece of bread into 4. Place on a lightly greased baking sheet and bake in a preheated moderately hot oven, 200°C (400°F), Gas Mark 6, for 12 to 15 minutes. Serve hot.
Serves 4 to 8

Asparagus and Tomato Pan Pizza; Pizza Turnovers; French Bread Pizza

DESSERTS AND BAKING

It is true to say that when you conjure up thoughts of Italian desserts, ice cream comes top of the list. Surprising really, for the Italians usually eat fresh fruit at the end of a meal and the special desserts and cakes they have become famous for are kept for special and important occasions like birthdays, Saints' days, Easter and Christmas.

That is not to say the Italians aren't partial to a scoop or two of ice cream piled high in a dessert glass; a soothing spoonful or two of creamy and warming Zabaglione; or a refreshing water ice or granita in the heat of the day or after a deal. Indeed, they have a number of interesting dessert dishes that are served on everyday occasions, many being based on a blend of soft cheeses like Ricotta and Mascarpone mixed with biscuits, liqueurs and fruit. Every Italian housewife has her own favourite recipe for Tiramisu (literally translated as pick-me-up) a sort of Italian trifle made with sponge cakes, fingers or ratafia biscuits, soft cheese, grated or powdered chocolate and lashings of brandy or Marsala. Cheese-cakes, large or small curd tarts and sponge-lined bombes are other ways in which the Italians use these readily-available ingredients to make desserts and cakes for finishing family-style meals.

SIMPLE STRAWBERRY ICE CREAM

250 g (8 oz) ripe
  strawberries
juice of ½ lemon
75 g (3 oz) icing
  sugar
200 ml (7 fl oz)
  whipping cream
75 g (3 oz) thick
  set natural yogurt
few strawberries,
  halved, to decorate

Purée the strawberries in a blender or food processor then stir in the lemon juice and icing sugar, mixing well. Whip the cream with the yogurt until thick but not stiff. Fold in the strawberry purée with a metal spoon. Place in a freezerproof container, cover and freeze until firm.

Transfer to a refrigerator about 1 hour before serving to allow the ice cream to soften slightly. Spoon into individual glass dishes and decorate with halved strawberries to serve.
Serves 4

MELON WITH GINGERED STRAWBERRIES

1 melon
icing sugar for dusting
½ teaspoon ground
  ginger
2 tablespoons honey
1 tablespoon lemon
  juice
375 g (12 oz)
  strawberries,
  hulled
mint sprigs, to
  decorate

Cut a 'lid' off the top of the melon and reserve. Scoop out the flesh with a melon baller, discarding the seeds; alternatively, cut into small balls. Reserve the shell. Sprinkle the melon flesh with the icing sugar, cover and chill until required. Mix the ginger with the honey and lemon juice and sprinkle over the strawberries, then cover and chill until required.

Just before serving, mix the melon and strawberries together, pile into the melon shell and cover with the 'lid'. Serve on a bed of crushed ice, decorated with mint sprigs.
Serves 4

COFFEE HAZELNUT ICE

100 g (3½ oz)
  hazelnuts, toasted
  and skinned
300 ml (½ pint)
  milk
4 egg yolks
75 g (3 oz) caster
  sugar
1 tablespoon instant
  coffee granules
175 ml (6 fl oz)
  whipping cream,
  whipped

Reserve a few nuts for decoration if liked; grind the remainder coarsely. Place the milk in a pan and bring almost to the boil. Cream together the egg yolks and sugar until pale, then gradually stir in the milk. Stir in the ground nuts.

Pour into a clean saucepan and heat gently, stirring, until the mixture is thick enough to coat the back of the spoon; do not allow to boil. Stir in the coffee granules, mixing well to blend. Cover and leave until cold, stirring occasionally.

Fold the cream into the coffee custard. Turn into individual freezerproof containers, cover and freeze until firm.

Transfer to the refrigerator 1 hour before serving to soften. Decorate with nuts if reserved, before serving.
Serves 4 to 5

BAKED STUFFED PEACHES

4 ripe peaches,
  halved and stoned
8 macaroons, crushed
4 blanched almonds,
  chopped
50 g (2 oz) sugar
25 g (1 oz) cocoa
  powder
7 tablespoons dry
  white wine
40 g (1½ oz) butter
flaked almonds, to
  decorate
icing sugar, to sprinkle

Scoop a little flesh from the centre of each peach half, chop and place in a bowl. Add the macaroon crumbs, almonds, half of the sugar, the cocoa and 1 tablespoon wine. Fill the peach halves with the mixture and top each with a small piece of butter.

Arrange in an ovenproof dish, pour over the remaining wine, sprinkle with the remaining sugar and top with a few flaked almonds to decorate. Bake in a preheated moderate oven, 180°C (350°F), Gas Mark 4, for 25 to 30 minutes or until the peaches are tender. Serve hot, sprinkled with icing sugar.
Serves 4

*Baked Stuffed Peaches; Simple Strawberry Ice Cream;
Melon with Gingered Strawberries; Coffee Hazelnut Ice*

ICED ANISETTE PEACHES

4 large fresh peaches,
    peeled, halved and
    stoned
8 small macaroons
about 50 ml (2 fl oz)
    anisette or orange-
    flavoured liqueur
caster sugar, to
    sprinkle

Place the peach halves in a pan with
just enough water to cover and
simmer gently until just tender, about
3–5 minutes. Remove with a slotted
spoon and drain on absorbent kitchen
paper.

Place the peach halves on a shallow
serving dish. Put a macaroon in the
centre of each and sprinkle with the
anisette liqueur. Sprinkle with sugar
to taste then cover and chill until very
cold, about 3 hours.

Serve well chilled with cream if
liked.

Serves 4

PEACH WATER ICE

125 g (4 oz) sugar
150 ml (¼ pint)
    water
4 large peaches,
    skinned and stoned
juice of 1 lemon

Place the sugar and water in a heavy-
based pan and heat gently to dissolve
the sugar. Bring to the boil and cook,
without stirring, for 5 minutes.
Remove from the heat and allow to
cool.

Purée the peaches in a blender or
food processor until smooth then mix
with the lemon juice. Stir in the cold
syrup and mix well. Pour into a
freezerproof container and freeze
until half frozen.

Remove from the freezer and
whisk to break down any large ice
crystals. Return to the freezer and
freeze until firm.

About 1 hour before required,
transfer to the refrigerator to soften
slightly before scooping to serve

Serves 4

COFFEE RUM GRANITA

75 g (3 oz) brown
    sugar
600 ml (1 pint) water
2 tablespoons instant
    coffee granules
4 tablespoons dark
    rum

Place the sugar and water in a heavy-
based pan and heat gently until the
sugar has dissolved. Bring to the boil
and cook, without stirring, for 5
minutes. Add the coffee, mixing well
and allow to cool.

Add the rum to the cooled coffee
mixture and mix well. Pour into a
freezerproof container and freeze
until half-frozen.

Remove from the freezer and
whisk to break down any large ice
crystals. Return to the freezer and
freeze until firm.

Leave at room temperature for
about 10 minutes, then stir until
crumbly. Spoon into tall chilled
glasses to serve.

Serves 4 to 6

LEFT: *Peach Water Ice; Coffee Rum Granita*

RIGHT: *Pears Italian Style*

PEARS ITALIAN STYLE

6 medium firm
  cooking pears
450 ml (¾ pint)
  medium Italian red
  or white wine
  (Barolo, for
  example)
125 g (4 oz) sugar
4 whole cloves
pinch of ground
  cinnamon

Peel the pears to remove their skins but keep the stalks intact. Stand upright in an ovenproof dish and pour over the wine. Sprinkle with the sugar, cloves and cinnamon.

Cover and bake in a preheated moderate oven, 160°C (325°F), Gas Mark 3, for 45 minutes or until the pears and the liquor is thick and syrupy. Serve hot or cold.
Serves 6

RICOTTA FRUIT TOPPER

16 sponge fingers
175 g (6 oz)
  raspberries
175 g (6 oz)
  strawberries,
  quartered
125 g (4 oz)
  blueberries
2 nectarines, stoned
  and chopped
1 teaspoon vanilla
  essence
2 tablespoons orange
  juice
1 tablespoon orange
  liqueur
625 g (1¼ lb) Ricotta
  cheese
40 g (1½ oz) icing
  sugar
6-8 Amaretti biscuits,
  crushed

Line the base of a medium-sized dessert dish (about 28 × 18 cm/11 × 7 inch) with the sponge fingers, breaking if necessary to fit.

Mix the raspberries with the strawberries, blueberries, nectarines, half of the vanilla essence, orange juice and orange liqueur. Spoon over the sponge fingers and spread evenly.

Beat the Ricotta with the remaining vanilla essence and icing sugar until smooth. Spread over the fruit mixture as evenly as possible.

Sprinkle with the Amaretti biscuit crumbs and chill for at least 2 hours before serving.
Serves 4 to 6

STRAWBERRY AND MACAROON ICE CREAM

150 g (5 oz) caster sugar
6 egg yolks
2 teaspoons cornflour
450 ml (¾ pint) milk
284 ml (½ pint) carton double cream
250 g (8 oz) strawberries, hulled
50 g (2 oz) macaroons, coarsely chopped

Whisk the sugar with the egg yolks and cornflour until creamy. Heat the milk and cream in a pan until boiling. Pour over the egg yolk mixture and whisk well to blend. Return to the pan and stir, over a low heat, until the mixture will coat the back of a spoon, about 2 minutes. Strain into a freezerproof container and allow to cool.

Crush the strawberries with a fork and stir into the cooled ice cream mixture. Freeze until half-frozen, about 1 hour, then beat to break down any large ice crystals. Stir in the macaroons, return to the freezer and freeze until firm, about 1-2 hours. Serve scooped into chilled glasses.
Serves 4 to 6

HONEY AND TOASTED PINE KERNEL ICE

150 g (5 oz) caster sugar
6 egg yolks
2 teaspoons cornflour
450 ml (¾ pint) milk
284 ml (½ pint) carton double cream
4 tablespoons set honey
25 g (1 oz) marzipan
3 drops of almond essence
50 g (2 oz) toasted pine kernels.

Whisk the sugar with the egg yolks and cornflour until creamy. Heat the milk and cream in a pan until boiling. Add the honey and marzipan and stir until dissolved, then add the almond essence. Return to the pan and stir, over a low heat, until the mixture will coat the back of a spoon, about 2 minutes. Strain into a freezerproof container and allow to cool.

Freeze until half-frozen, about 1 hour, then beat to break down any large ice crystals. Stir in the toasted pine kernels, return to the freezer and freeze until firm, about 1-2 hours. Serve scooped into chilled dessert glasses.
Serves 4 to 6

CHOCOLATE ORANGE BOMBES

175 g (6 oz) plain chocolate, broken into pieces
3 tablespoons water
2 eggs, separated
125 g (4 oz) caster sugar
284 ml (10 fl oz) double cream
2 tablespoons orange liqueur
75 g (3 oz) meringues, broken into pieces
TO SERVE:
1 quantity Bitter Mocha Sauce (see page 143)

Place the chocolate and water in a small pan and heat gently until melted. Stir in the egg yolks and leave to cool.

Whisk the egg whites until they form stiff peaks, then gradually whisk in the sugar.

Whip the cream and liqueur together until soft peaks form, then fold in the chocolate mixture. Carefully fold in the whisked egg whites and broken meringues.

Turn into a 1.5 litre (2½ pint) pudding basin, or into eight 175 ml (6 fl oz) individual moulds, cover with foil, seal and freeze until firm.

Dip each mould into warm water and turn out onto a serving dish. Pour some of the chocolate sauce over the top and serve the rest separately.
Serves 8

RASPBERRY AND MERINGUE ICE CREAM

250 g (8 oz) raspberries
juice of ½ lemon
50 g (2 oz) icing sugar
284 ml (½ pint) carton whipping cream
50 g (2 oz) meringues
TO SERVE:
whipped cream
chocolate leaves
fresh raspberries

Crush the raspberries with a fork until almost smooth then stir in the lemon juice and icing sugar, mixing well. Whip the cream until it stands in soft peaks. Break the meringue into small pieces. Fold the cream and meringue pieces into the strawberry mixture with a metal spoon. Place in a small freezerproof loaf dish, cover and freeze until firm.

Transfer to a refrigerator about 1 hour before serving to allow the ice cream to soften slightly. .Cut into slices and place on individual serving plates. Serve with whipped cream, chocolate leaves and a few fresh raspberries.
Serves 4

RUM AND CHOCOLATE RICOTTA MOUSSE

500 g (1 lb) Ricotta cheese
40 g (1½ oz) icing sugar
1 tablespoon unsweetened cocoa powder
1 teaspoon vanilla essence
1 tablespoon dark rum
2 egg whites
pinch of cream of tartar
cocoa powder
powdered chocolate, to decorate

Place the Ricotta, 1 tablespoon of the icing sugar, the cocoa powder, vanilla essence and rum in a food processor or blender and purée until smooth.

Whisk the egg whites until foamy then whisk in the cream of tartar. Gradually beat in the remaining icing sugar and whisk until the mixture stands in firm peaks and is thick and glossy. Fold into the chocolate and rum mixture with a metal spoon.

Spoon into four individual dessert glasses and chill thoroughly. Sprinkle with cocoa powder before serving.
Serves 4

CHESTNUT BIANCO

500 g (1 lb) chestnuts
2 tablespoons milk
175 g (6 oz) icing sugar, sifted
pinch of salt
142 ml (¼ pint) carton double cream
2 tablespoons brandy or Strega liqueur

Cut a cross into the pointed end of each chestnut with a sharp knife. Place in a pan, cover with water, bring to the boil, reduce the heat and simmer for 15 minutes. Drain and while still hot peel off the shells and skins.

Return to the pan, cover with cold water, bring to the boil, reduce the heat and simmer for 45 minutes or until soft. Drain, place in a blender or food processor with the milk, sugar and salt and purée until smooth. Spoon into dessert glasses and chill until required.

To serve, whip the cream with the brandy or liqueur until it stands in soft peaks. Swirl on top of the chestnut mixture to serve.
Serves 4

RIGHT: *Chestnut Bianco*

LEFT: *Chocolate Orange Bombes*

CHOCOLATE CHERRY DOME

1 × 20 cm (8 inch) chocolate sponge sandwich cake
6 tablespoons Kirsch
450 ml (¾ pint) double cream
40 g (1½ oz) icing sugar, sifted
75 g (3 oz) plain chocolate, chopped
175 g (6 oz) black cherries, pitted
1 tablespoon cocoa powder, sifted

Split the sponge in half and line a 1.2 litre (2 pint) pudding basin with one layer, shaping it to fit. Sprinkle the sides with 4 tablespoons of Kirsch; set aside.

Whip the cream until it forms soft peaks. Fold in 25 g (1 oz) of the icing sugar, the chocolate, cherries and remaining Kirsch. Spoon into the basin and top with the remaining sponge. Cover with a plate and chill for 2 to 3 hours.

Run a palette knife around the sides of the bowl and turn out. Sprinkle with the remaining icing sugar and cocoa powder to make a pattern.
Serves 6 to 8

ITALIAN NUT DOME

1 × 20 cm (8 inch) sponge sandwich cake
2 tablespoons brandy
4 tablespoons orange juice
125 g (4 oz) plain chocolate
284 ml (½ pint) carton double cream
8 tablespoons icing sugar, sifted
50 g (2 oz) blanched almonds, toasted and chopped
50 g (2 oz) hazelnuts, toasted and chopped

Cut the cake into pointed slices and use to line a 900 ml (1½ pint) base-lined pudding basin; reserve 3 or 4 slices for the top.

Mix the brandy and orange juice together and sprinkle over the cake. Chop 25 g (1 oz) of the chocolate and set aside. Melt the remainder in a heatproof bowl over a pan of simmering water.

Whip the cream and half the icing sugar together to form stiff peaks. Fold in the nuts and divide the mixture in half. Fold the chopped chocolate into one half and the melted chocolate into the other. Spread the chopped chocolate mixture over the sponge, then fill the centre with the melted chocolate mixture.

Use the reserved cake slices to cover the surface of the cake. Cover with foil and freeze until firm.

Turn out onto a chilled serving plate and place in the refrigerator 30 minutes before serving to soften slightly. Dust thickly with the remaining icing sugar.
Serves 6 to 8

ABOVE: *Italian Nut Dome*

LEFT: *Chocolate Cherry Dome*

ORANGE AND VANILLA ICE CREAM BOMBE

1.5 litres (2½ pints) vanilla ice cream
100 g (3½ oz) sponge fingers
6 tablespoons orange juice
6 tablespoons Cointreau
3 egg yolks
50 g (2 oz) caster sugar
finely grated rind of 2 oranges
568 ml (1 pint) carton double cream
few drops of vanilla essence
a little grated chocolate
orange slices, to decorate

Line a 1.5 litre (2½ pint) pudding basin with clingfilm. Remove the ice cream from the freezer and allow to soften slightly. Using three-quarters of the ice cream, line the pudding basin with a 2.5 cm (1 inch) thick layer of ice cream, smoothing it as much as possible. Return the basin and remaining ice cream to the freezer and freeze until firm.

Meanwhile, break the sponge fingers into small pieces and place in a shallow dish. Sprinkle over the orange juice and Cointreau. Cover and leave to stand for 10-15 minutes until the sponge fingers have absorbed the liquid. Put the egg yolks, sugar and orange rind in a large mixing bowl and whisk until thick and creamy. Whisk the soaked sponge fingers into the egg yolk mixture.

Whip half of the cream until it stands in soft peaks. Fold into the egg yolk mixture. Pour into the centre of the ice cream-lined pudding basin. Cover and freeze until firm.

Slightly soften the remaining vanilla ice cream then spread over the top of the frozen orange cream, smoothing the top well. Return to the freezer and freeze until firm.

To serve, invert the bombe onto a chilled serving plate, removing any clingfilm. Whip the remaining cream with the vanilla essence until it stands in soft peaks. Place in a piping bag fitted with a star-shaped nozzle and pipe small stars all over the ice cream bombe. Sprinkle with grated chocolate. Serve at once, decorated with orange slices.
Serves 6 to 8

CHOCOLATE RATAFIA ICE

175 g (6 oz) plain chocolate, broken into pieces
142 ml (¼ pint) carton single cream
2 tablespoons brandy
284 ml (½ pint) carton double cream, whipped
50 g (2 oz) ratafias, finely crushed
50 g (2 oz) crystallized fruit
TO FINISH:
40 g (1½ oz) ratafias, crushed
4 tablespoons double cream, whipped
8 chocolate circles (see box tip page 142)

Place the chocolate and single cream in a small pan and heat gently until melted. Stir well until smooth, then leave until cool.

Whisk the brandy and chocolate mixture into the whipped cream, then fold in the ratafias and fruit. Spoon into a 500 g (1 lb) loaf tin and smooth the surface. Cover with foil, seal and freeze overnight.

Turn upside down over a chilled serving plate and rub the tin with a cloth wrung out in very hot water until the ice cream drops out.

Press the ratafia crumbs over the top and sides of the ice cream. Pipe the cream down the centre and decorate with the chocolate circles.
Serves 8

Right: Chocolate Ratafia Ice

BRANDIED CARAMEL ORANGES

6 oranges
300 g (10 oz) granulated sugar
350 ml (12 fl oz) water
2 tablespoons brandy

Remove the peel from 1 of the oranges and cut into thin julienne strips. Place in a pan with water to cover and bring to the boil and cook until tender, about 5 minutes. Drain well.

Remove the peel and pith from all of the oranges then slice the flesh into thin rounds. Place the sugar and 300 ml (½ pint) of the water in a pan and heat until dissolved. Bring to the boil, add the orange strips and cook, uncovered, for 10 minutes. Remove the strips with a slotted spoon and set aside. Continue to boil the syrup until it caramelises to a rich golden colour. Remove from the heat and add the remaining water. Return to the heat and cook until smooth and dissolved. Allow to cool then stir in the brandy.

Arrange the orange slices on a large serving plate and pour over the cooled syrup. Top with the orange strips and chill thoroughly before serving.
Serves 4

TIRAMISU

16 sponge fingers
60 ml (2½ fl oz) dark rum
2 tablespoons brandy or Marsala
125 ml (4 fl oz) strong, cold black coffee
10 small macaroons
3 tablespoons apricot jam
425 g (14 oz) Mascarpone cheese
2 eggs, separated
4 tablespoons icing sugar
125 g (4 oz) powdered or finely grated chocolate

Bake the sponge fingers in a preheated moderately hot oven, 190°C (375°F), Gas Mark 5 for 10-15 minutes, until very crisp and dry.

Mix half of the rum with the brandy and coffee. Dip the sponge fingers into this mixture then layer in a shallow serving dish.

Spread the macaroons with the jam and arrange over the top. Beat the cheese with the egg yolks, sugar and remaining rum. Whisk the egg whites until they stand in stiff peaks. Fold into the cheese mixture with a metal spoon. Spoon over the macaroons then sprinkle with the chocolate. Cover and chill overnight or for at least 6-8 hours.
Serves 4

RED MOUNTAINS

3 pomegranates
juice of 1 lemon
6 tablespoons granulated sugar
6 tablespoons orange liqueur or brandy
284 ml (½ pint) carton whipping cream
2 tablespoons icing sugar

Remove the skin and pith from the pomegranates to release the fleshy seeds. Place in a bowl with the lemon juice, sugar and liqueur or brandy. Mix gently but thoroughly to dissolve the sugar. Cover and chill for at least 1 hour.

To serve, whip the cream and the icing sugar until it stands in soft peaks. Pipe or spoon a small mound onto or into 6 dessert plates or glasses. Spoon over an equal quantity of the marinated pomegranate and serve at once.
Serves 6

CHOCOLATE MARSALA PEACHES

125 ml (4 fl oz) water
75 ml (3 fl oz) Marsala
50 g (2 oz) sugar
4 peaches, peeled, halved and stoned
SAUCE:
125 g (4 oz) caster sugar
4 tablespoons Marsala
2 egg yolks
pinch of salt
50 g (2 oz) plain chocolate
4 tablespoons milk
flaked toasted almonds, to decorate

Place the water, Marsala and sugar in a pan and slowly bring to the boil to dissolve the sugar. Add the peaches, reduce the heat and simmer until tender, about 5 minutes.

Meanwhile, to make the sauce, mix the sugar with the Marsala, egg yolks and salt. Heat the chocolate and milk in a bowl over a pan of hot water until melted. Gradually beat in the Marsala mixture and cook until lightly thickened, about 5 minutes, stirring constantly.

Remove the peaches from the syrup with a slotted spoon and place in serving dishes. Spoon over the sauce and sprinkle with the almonds to decorate. Serve warm, or allow to cool and serve chilled.

Serves 4

GIPSY ORANGES

2 oranges
142 ml (¼ pint) carton whipping cream
150 g (5oz) thick set yogurt or fromage frais
1 egg white
50 g (2 oz) plain chocolate
125 g (4 oz) ratafias or small macaroons

Peel the oranges over a bowl with a knife, removing all the white pith. Divide into segments. Whip the cream until it stands in stiff peaks, then whip in the yogurt and any orange juice collected. Whisk the egg white until it stands in stiff peaks. Fold into the cream mixture with a metal spoon. Roughly chop the chocolate.

In pretty serving dishes, tall glasses or chocolate cases, layer the cream with the orange segments, ratafias and pieces of chocolate, saving a few orange segments and chocolate pieces to decorate the tops. Chill lightly before serving.

Serves 4

BAKED CHEESECAKE

75 g (3 oz) butter
125 g (4 oz) caster sugar
grated rind and juice of 1 lemon
300 g (10 oz) curd cheese
2 eggs, separated
50 g (2 oz) ground almonds
25 g (1 oz) semolina
50 g (2 oz) sultanas
sifted icing sugar for dredging

Cream the butter, sugar and lemon rind together until light and fluffy. Beat in the cheese gradually, then mix in the egg yolks and beat thoroughly. Add the almonds, semolina, sultanas and lemon juice and mix well. Whisk the egg whites until stiff and carefully fold into the cheese mixture.

Spoon into a lined and greased 20 cm (8 inch) loose-bottomed cake tin and bake in a preheated moderate oven, 180°C (350°F), Gas Mark 4 for 50 to 60 minutes. Turn off the heat and leave the cheesecake in the oven until cold.

Turn out and sprinkle with icing sugar.

Serves 6 to 8

Baked Cheesecake

ITALIAN STRAWBERRY MERINGUE TRIFLE

250 g (8 oz) sponge
cake
175 g (6 oz)
strawberries, sliced
7-8 tablespoons
dark rum
750 ml (1¼ pints)
custard
200 g (7 oz)
macaroons, crushed
4 egg whites
5 tablespoons caster
sugar
1 tablespoon sweet
vermouth

Break the sponge cake into pieces and place in a decorative ovenproof dessert dish. Add the strawberries and sprinkle over 5 tablespoons of the rum. Cover with half of the custard. Mix the crushed macaroons with the remaining rum to soften slightly.

Whisk the egg whites until they stand in stiff peaks then fold in the sugar and sweet vermouth with a metal spoon. Spoon on top of the custard then cover with the remaining custard. Sprinkle with the soaked macaroon crumbs.

Bake in a preheated moderately hot oven 190°C (375°F), Gas Mark 5 for 20 minutes or until golden. Serve at once.
Serves 6

SPEEDY CHOCOLATE AND ORANGE SAUCE

125 g (4 oz) plain
chocolate-orange
cake covering,
broken into pieces
juice of 1 orange
1 × 170 g (6 oz) can
evaporated milk
2 tablespoons Grand
Marnier

Place all the ingredients, except the Grand Marnier, in a small pan and heat gently until melted. Bring to the boil and simmer for 3 minutes, then add the Grand Marnier. Serve warm or cold, with ices and chocolate sponge.
Makes 450 ml (¾ pint)

CHILLED RICOTTA PUDDING

425 g (14 oz) Ricotta
or cream cheese
50 g (2 oz) icing
sugar
3 egg yolks
4 tablespoons dark
rum
1 tablespoon Marsala
200 ml (7 fl oz)
whipping cream
langue de chat or
sponge fingers, to
serve

Beat the Ricotta or cream cheese with the icing sugar and egg yolks until smooth and creamy. Stir in the rum and Marsala, mixing well.

Whip the cream until it stands in stiff peaks then fold into the cheese mixture with a metal spoon. Pour into 4 dessert glasses and chill for at least 3 hours.

Serve lightly chilled with langue de chat or sponge finger biscuits.
Serves 4

CHOCOLATE DECORATIONS

When it comes to prettying up a dessert the simplest ideas are usually the most effective and popular. Chocolate curls, splinters, buttons and vermicelli are all simple and delicious but for a more professional finish chocolate leaves and shapes are hard to beat. To make chocolate leaves, coat the underside of small rose leaves with melted chocolate using a fine paintbrush. Leave to set, chocolate side up, then carefully peel away the leaf. To make chocolate shapes, spread the melted chocolate on baking parchment and leave until just firm but not too hard. Cut into rounds using pastry cutters and into squares or rectangles by using a sharp knife and ruler. Leave until hard, then carefully lift the paper and peel away from the chocolate. Chocolate decorations can be stored in an airtight container in a cool place for several weeks.

BITTER MOCHA SAUCE

175 g (6 oz) plain
  chocolate, broken
  into pieces
150 ml (¼ pint)
  water
2 teaspoons instant
  coffee granules
50 g (2 oz) brown
  sugar crystals

Place all the ingredients in a small pan and heat gently until the sugar crystals have dissovled. Bring to the boil and simmer gently for 10 minutes. Serve hot or cold, with ice cream, sponge puddings, pears and profiteroles.
Makes 300 ml (½ pint)

SPECIAL FUDGE SAUCE

1 × 170 g (6 oz) can
  evaporated milk
50 g (2 oz) plain
  chocolate, broken
  into pieces
50 g (2 oz) soft dark
  brown sugar
1 tablespoon Tia
  Maria

Place the evaporated milk, chocolate and sugar in a pan; heat gently until the sugar has dissolved. Bring to the boil and simmer for 3 minutes. Remove from the heat and stir in the Tia Maria. Serve warm or cold.
Makes 250 ml (8 fl oz)

MINT-CHOC SAUCE

175 g (6 oz) plain
  chocolate, in pieces
284 ml (½ pint)
  carton single cream
50 g (2 oz) caster
  sugar
1 teaspoon
  peppermint essence

Place the chocolate, cream and sugar in a small pan and heat gently until the sugar has dissolved. Bring to the boil and simmer for 2 minutes, then stir in the peppermint essence. Serve hot or cold, with ice cream.
Makes 450 ml (¾ pint)

Bitter Mocha Sauce; Speedy Chocolate and Orange Sauce; Special Fudge Sauce; Mint-Choc Sauce

CHOCOLATE FIG LOAF

125 g (4 oz) sugar
3 eggs
125 g (4 oz)
   hazelnuts, toasted
   and chopped
75 g (3 oz) flaked
   almonds, chopped
125 g (4 oz) dried
   figs, coarsely
   chopped
125 g (4 oz) mixed
   chopped peel
75 g (3 oz) plain
   chocolate, coarsely
   grated
200 g (7 oz) self-
   raising flour

Whisk the sugar with the eggs until very thick and pale. Add the hazelnuts, almonds, figs, peel and chocolate and fold in gently with a metal spoon.

Sift the flour over the nut mixture then fold in gently with a metal spoon. Transfer to a greased 20 × 10 cm (8 × 4 inch) loaf tin. Bake in a preheated moderately hot oven, 190°C (375°F), Gas Mark 5 for about 1 hour or until cooked and golden. Allow to cool slightly in the tin before turning out to cool on a wire rack. Cut into slices to serve.
Makes one 20 × 10 cm (8 × 4 inch) loaf

HAZELNUT AND LEMON BISCUITS

50 g (2 oz) butter
4 tablespoons caster
   sugar
2 tablespoons sweet
   white wine
grated rind of 1 lemon
1 egg, separated
125 ml (4 fl oz) olive
   oil
25 g (1 oz)
   hazelnuts,
   chopped
200 g (7 oz) plain
   flour

Cream the butter with half of the sugar until light and fluffy. Beat in the wine and lemon rind, then the egg yolk and olive oil. Add the hazelnuts and stir well to mix.

Gradually add the flour, mixing to a smooth but pliable dough. Wrap in foil and chill for 30 minutes.

Roll out the dough on a lightly floured surface to 5 mm (¼ inch) thickness and stamp out about 15 rounds with a 5 cm (2 inch) round biscuit cutter. Place on a greased baking sheet. Lightly whisk the egg white with a fork then brush over the tops of the biscuits. Sprinkle with the remaining caster sugar.

Bake in a preheated moderate oven, 180°C (350°F), Gas Mark 4 for 15 minutes or until golden. Allow to cool on a wire rack. Store in an airtight tin.
Makes about 15

ITALIAN FRUIT CAKE

250 g (8 oz) self-
   raising flour
50 g (2 oz) sugar
125 ml (4 fl oz) milk
4 tablespoons
   Marsala
150 ml (¼ pint)
   olive oil
grated rind of 1 small
   orange
50 g (2 oz) sultanas
25 g (1 oz) raisins
25 g (1 oz) chopped
   mixed peel
25 g (1 oz) chopped
   mixed nuts

Sift the flour into a bowl, add the sugar and mix well. Make a well in the centre and add the milk and Marsala. Mix as much of the flour and sugar mixture into the milk and Marsala as you can.

Heat the oil and orange rind in a small pan until very hot then add to the flour mixture and beat to a smooth consistency. Add the sultanas, raisins, peel, nuts and mix.

Spoon into a greased 18 cm (7 inch) round cake tin and level the surface. Bake in a preheated moderate oven, 180°C (350°F), Gas Mark 4 for about 45 minutes or until the cake is golden and firm to the touch. Allow to cool in the tin, then turn out to cool on a wire rack. Store in an airtight tin.
Makes one 18 cm (7 inch) cake

MELON AND PLUM TART

PASTRY:
250 g (8 oz) plain
   flour
pinch of salt
125 g (4 oz) butter
1 large egg (size 2),
   beaten
1 tablespoon water
beaten egg, to glaze
caster sugar
FILLING:
567 g (1 lb 3 oz) can
   plums, drained
1 small melon,
   weighing about
   750 g (1½ lb),
   skinned, seeded
   and cut into 2.5 cm
   (1 inch) cubes
2 tablespoons sugar
½ teaspoon ground
   ginger

To make the pastry, sift the flour and the salt into a bowl. Rub in the butter or margarine until the mixture resembles fine breadcrumbs. Stir in the egg and water and bind to a firm but pliable dough. Knead until smooth.

Place the plums and melon in the base of a 20 cm (8 inch) pie plate or shallow pie dish. Sprinkle the sugar and ginger on top.

Roll out the pastry on a lightly floured surface to a round 2.5 cm (1 inch) larger than the dish and dampen the edges of the dish. Cover the pie with pastry and flute the edges to seal. Decorate the tart with any pastry trimmings. Glaze with beaten egg and sprinkle with sugar. Bake in a preheated moderately hot oven, 200°C (400°F), Gas Mark 6 for 25-30 minutes until the pastry is crisp and golden.
Serves 6

HONEYED NUT CAKE

75 g (3 oz) hazelnuts
75 g (3 oz) blanched
  almonds, coarsely
  chopped
175 g (6 oz) candied
  peel, finely
  chopped
25 g (1 oz) cocoa
  powder
50 g (2 oz) plain
  flour, sifted
½ teaspoon ground
  cinnamon
¼ teaspoon ground
  mixed spice
125 g (4 oz) caster
  sugar
125 g (4 oz) clear
  honey
TO FINISH:
2 tablespoons icing
  sugar
1 teaspoon ground
  cinnamon

Spread the nuts on a baking sheet and place under a preheated moderate grill until the skins split, shaking frequently. Turn into a rough towel and rub off the loose skins. Grind the hazelnuts coarsely.

Place the hazelnuts, almonds, candied peel, cocoa powder, flour and spices in a mixing bowl and stir well.

Put the sugar and honey in a pan and heat gently until the sugar has melted. Boil gently until a little of the mixture forms a soft ball when dropped into a cup of cold water. Remove from the heat and stir in the dry ingredients.

Press into a lined and greased 20 cm (8 inch) loose-bottomed flan tin so that the mixture is no more than 1 cm (½ inch) thick. Bake in a preheated cool oven 150°C (300°F), Gas Mark 2, for 30 to 35 minutes.

Remove from the flan tin and allow to cool. Peel off the lining paper and transfer to a serving plate. Mix the icing sugar with the cinnamon and sift over the 'cake'. Serve cut into wedges.
Serves 8 to 10

Honeyed Nut Cake

SICILIAN CHOCOLATE AND GINGER CHEESECAKE

BASE:
*175 g (6 oz)
chocolate digestive
biscuits, crushed*
75 g (3 oz) butter
TOPPING:
*625 g (1¼ lb) Ricotta
cheese*
*175 g (6 oz) icing
sugar*
*1 teaspoon vanilla
essence*
*2 tablespoons Crème
de Cacao*
*50 g (2 oz) plain
chocolate, grated*
*25 g (1 oz) stem
ginger, chopped*
*125 ml (4 fl oz)
double cream
chocolate curls and
chopped stem
ginger, to decorate*

To make the base, place the biscuit crumbs in a bowl. Melt the butter in a pan, add to the biscuit crumbs and mix well to coat. Press onto the base of a 20 cm (8 inch) springform tin and chill to set, about 15 minutes.

Meanwhile, to make the filling, beat the cheese with the icing sugar, vanilla essence and Crème de Cacao until smooth. Add the chocolate and stem ginger and stir well to mix. Spoon over the prepared base, level the surface and chill for at least 6 hours.

Whip the cream until it stands in soft peaks. Spread over the top of the cheesecake. Transfer from the tin to a serving plate and decorate the top with chocolate curls and chopped stem ginger. Serve cut into wedges.
Serves 6

ITALIAN BISCUIT SUNDAE

8 macaroons
*50 g (2 oz) toasted
almonds, finely
chopped*
*8 tablespoons sweet
white wine or
vermouth*
*4 slices vanilla ice
cream*
*4 Amaretti biscuits,
crushed*
*toasted flaked
almonds, to
decorate*

Coarsely crush the macaroons and mix with the chopped almonds. Divide evenly between 4 individual dessert glasses. Sprinkle over the wine or vermouth and leave for a few minutes to soak.

Place a slice of the ice cream on top of the biscuit and wine mixture then sprinkle with the crushed Amaretti. Decorate with toasted flaked almonds and serve at once.
Serves 4

HAZELNUT COOKIES

75 g (3 oz) hazelnuts
125 g (4 oz) butter
*40 g (1½ oz) icing
sugar*
*1½ tablespoons clear
honey*
*125 g (4 oz) plain
flour*
icing sugar for dusting

Spread the nuts on a baking sheet and place under a preheated moderate grill until the skins split, shaking frequently. Turn into a rough towel and rub off the loose skins. Grind coarsely.

Cream the butter, sugar and honey together until fluffy. Add the flour and nuts and mix to a dough.

With lightly floured hands, shape teaspoonfuls of the mixture into ovals and place about 5 cm (2 inches) apart on lightly oiled baking sheets.

Bake in a preheated moderate oven, 180°C (350°F), Gas Mark 4, for about 15 minutes, until firm. Cool slightly, then roll in icing sugar. Transfer to a wire rack and leave until cold. Store in an airtight container.
Makes about 24

ITALIAN SOUFFLÉ OMELETTE

2 eggs, separated
2 teaspoons cold
   water
2 teaspoons caster
   sugar
¼ teaspoon vanilla
   essence
15 g (½ oz) butter
icing sugar for
   sprinkling
FILLING:
2 scoops Neapolitan
   ice cream
2 teaspoons chopped
   nuts

Whisk together the egg yolks, water, sugar and vanilla essence until pale and creamy. Whisk the egg whites until just stiff enough to stand in peaks, then gently fold both mixtures together with a metal spoon.

Melt the butter in a preheated pan until just beginning to sizzle, taking care that it does not burn. Add the egg mixture and spread evenly. Cook gently for about 2 minutes until set around the edge, then place under a preheated moderately hot grill for 1 to 2 minutes until the surface feels firm to the touch and looks puffy.

Alternatively, place in a preheated moderately hot oven, 200°C (400°F), for 3 to 4 minutes.

Slide the unfolded omelette onto a serving plate, sprinkle with the icing sugar, top with the ice cream, sprinkle with the nuts and serve immediately.

Serves 1

NEAPOLITAN CURD TART

PASTRY:
250 g (8 oz) plain
   flour
pinch of salt
75 g (3 oz) caster
   sugar
125 g (4 oz) butter,
   softened
finely grated zest of
   ½ lemon
2 egg yolks
FILLING:
375 g (12 oz) Ricotta
   or curd cheese
75 g (3 oz) caster
   sugar
3 eggs, beaten
50 g (2 oz) blanched
   almonds, chopped
75 g (3 oz) chopped
   mixed peel
finely grated zest of
   ½ orange
finely grated zest of
   ½ lemon
¼ teaspoon vanilla
   essence
icing sugar to decorate

To make the pastry, sift the flour with the salt into a bowl. Add the sugar, mix then make a well in the centre. Add the butter, lemon zest and egg yolks. Gradually draw the flour into the centre, with the fingertips, and mix to a firm but pliable dough. Cover and chill for 1 hour.

Meanwhile, to make the filling, mix the cheese with the sugar. Gradually beat in the eggs to make a smooth mixture. Fold in the almonds, peel, fruits zests and vanilla essence.

Roll out the pastry and use to line a 18 to 20 cm (7 to 8 inch) flan ring standing on a baking sheet. Fill the flan with the cheese mixture, spreading evenly.

Bake in a preheated moderate oven, 180°C (350°F), Gas Mark 4 for 45 minutes. Cool on a wire rack. Sprinkle with icing sugar to decorate.

Serves 6 to 8

Neapolitan Curd Tart

BASIC RECIPES

It is said that the Italians live to eat rather than eat to live and their repertoire of recipes reflects this. A love of all good things means that the Italian cook places great emphasis and value on a good basic stock and sauce, home-made pasta and pizza dough and carefully blended butters and mayonnaises for countless uses. So much so that any self-respecting cook would have at hand any number of fresh, chilled or frozen sauces for pasta, stock for risotto, butters for meat grills and plainly-boiled vegetables, marinades for meat, poultry and fish grills.

The recipes that follow can arm you with such a convenient 'storecupboard' of basics. Many can be made well ahead then chilled and sometimes frozen for convenience. Some, like Rich Meat Sauce, Béchamel Sauce, Mayonnaise and Speedy Tomato Sauce will prove indispensable and are worth making in bulk. Others, like Chicken Liver Sauce, Piquant Green Sauce and Anchovy Butter may well become family favourites. Not surprisingly, if you become a pasta and pizza lover then the recipes for home-made egg pasta and pizza dough will be invaluable.

HOME-MADE EGG PASTA

500 g (1 lb) plain
 white or
 wholemeal flour
2 large eggs (size
 1-2)
1 teaspoon oil
½ teaspoon salt
3-4 tablespoons water
 (approximately)

Sift the flour into a heap on a work surface and make a well in the centre. Put the eggs, oil and salt into the well and mix together with the fingers. Gradually work in the flour to form a crumbly dough. Knead to a firm but pliable dough, adding a little water as necessary. Knead for 10 minutes, until smooth and elastic. Cover and leave to rest for 1 hour.

Roll out the dough on a lightly floured surface, first in one direction and then in the other, continuing until the pasta is paper thin. Shape and use as required (see below).

Makes 500 g (1 lb) quantity

Pasta Verdi (Green Pasta)

Follow the above recipe, adding 125 g (4 oz) cooked sieved spinach (weighed after having been squeezed very dry) with the eggs but reducing the flour to 375 g (12 oz) and omitting the water.

Shaping Pasta

Stuffed Pasta: The dough should be used immediately, without drying.

Flat and Ribbon Pasta: Dust the dough lightly with flour and leave to dry for 15 to 20 minutes, but do not allow to become brittle. Cut flat pasta into shapes and roll ribbon pasta into a loose Swiss roll and cut across into strips as illustrated.

Cooking Pasta

Home-made Pasta: Put the pasta into a large pan containing 2.25 to 2.75 litres (4 to 5 pints) fast boiling water and 1½ tablespoons salt. Stir well, then boil steadily, uncovered, for 3 to 5 minutes until *al dente* – just tender but firm to the bite. Test frequently to avoid overcooking, as pasta continues to soften until you eat it. The moment it is done, tip the pasta into a colander, drain thoroughly and serve immediately.

Manufactured Pasta: As above, but follow the packet directions because cooking times are longer for manufactured pastas and vary considerably for different shapes and brands.

Never break up long pasta such as spaghetti unless stated; simply bend it into the pan as it softens.

Quantities:

Allow 75 to 125 g (3 to 4 oz) pasta per person for a main course, 50 g (2 oz) for a starter.

PIZZA DOUGH

There are many ways of making basic pizza doughs. The one recommended is the traditional bread dough, which is made with strong flour and yeast.

If time is short, a packet of commercially made bread mix can be used instead. It is equally good and has the advantage of being quick and very easy. Follow the packet instructions exactly, then roll out evenly and use as indicated in each recipe.

A range of ready-made pizza bases and jars of pizza sauce are available from many supermarkets – a definite boon when you need an instant snack.

*200 g (7 oz) plain
  flour
1 teaspoon salt
1 packet easy blend
  dried yeast
1 tablespoon olive oil
150 ml (¼ pint)
  warm water*

Mix the flour, salt and yeast in a large bowl. Add the oil and water and knead to a soft, elastic dough; this will take about 8 minutes by hand or 4 to 5 minutes in a food processor or electric blender. Cover and leave to rise in a warm place for 2½ to 3 hours, until doubled in size.

Makes one 25 cm (10 inch) pizza

To Roll Out Pizza Dough
Place the dough on a floured surface and knead lightly. Roll out to a 25-30 cm (10-12 inch) circle, about 5 mm (¼ inch) thick, turning the dough as it is rolled to prevent shrinking. Using the fingertips, push some of the dough from the centre towards the edge, making the edge about twice as thick as the rest of the circle.

Place the dough on a lightly floured piece of circular cardboard and proceed as directed in each recipe. Assembling the pizza on a cardboard circle makes it easier to transfer to the baking sheet.

If the recipe states 'place the pizza on a hot baking sheet', put the baking sheet in the oven to warm while preheating the oven. Leave it in there until it is really hot. This is most important, as it ensures that the pizza will have a crisp base and that the top and base will cook evenly.

BÉCHAMEL SAUCE

40 g (1½ oz) butter
40 g (1½ oz) plain
  flour
600 ml (1 pint) hot
  milk
salt and pepper
grated nutmeg

Melt the butter in a saucepan, add the flour and cook, stirring, for 1 minute. Remove from the heat and gradually stir in the milk.

Return to the heat and cook, stirring, until thickened. Simmer for 3 minutes. Season with salt, pepper and nutmeg to taste.

Makes about 600 ml (1 pint)

NOTE: For additional flavour, add a bay leaf to the milk before heating. Remove before adding the milk to the sauce.

MAYONNAISE

2 large egg yolks
  (size 1-2)
1 teaspoon salt
2-3 teaspoons lemon
  juice
200 ml (7 fl oz) olive
  oil

Have all the ingredients at room temperature.

Put the egg yolks into a small basin, add the salt and 1 teaspoon of the lemon juice and mix thoroughly. Add the oil drop by drop, stirring constantly, until the sauce becomes thick and shiny. Add the rest of the oil in a thin stream, stirring constantly. Add lemon juice to taste.

Makes about 300 ml (½ pint)

TUNA FISH MAYONNAISE

200 ml (⅓ pint)
  Mayonnaise (see
  below)
1 × 99 g (3½ oz)
  can tuna fish
3 anchovy fillets
1 tablespoon lemon
  juice

Put the Mayonnaise into a blender or food processor, add the remaining ingredients and work until smooth. If necessary, thin to a coating consistency by adding a little cold water.

Alternatively, rub the undrained tuna fish and the anchovies through a sieve into a bowl. Add the egg yolks and proceed as for Mayonnaise (see below).

Use to coat hard-boiled eggs, sliced cold chicken, turkey or veal, or to stuff tomatoes.

Makes about 300 ml (½ pint)

PIQUANT GREEN SAUCE

2 shallots
1 clove garlic
1 pickled gherkin
1 tablespoon capers
40 g (1½ oz) parsley
2 tablespoons lemon
  juice
6 tablespoons olive
  oil
salt and pepper

Put all the ingredients in a blender or food processor and work until smooth, seasoning with salt and pepper to taste.

Alternatively, chop the first 5 ingredients together very finely. Stir in the lemon juice and oil, and season with salt and pepper to taste.

Serve with hot or cold boiled meat, fish or poultry.

Makes about 200 ml (7 fl oz)

ANCHOVY BUTTER

6 anchovy fillets
125 g (4 oz) unsalted
  butter, softened
1 teaspoon anchovy
  essence

Rinse the anchovies in cold water; dry thoroughly. Chop finely, then rub through a sieve. Beat into the butter with the anchovy essence.

Serve with grilled fish and herrings.

Makes 125 g (4 oz)

PIQUANT TOMATO SAUCE

1 kg (2 lb) tomatoes,
  roughly chopped
4 shallots, chopped
½ carrot, grated
4 tablespoons orange
  juice
1 teaspoon grated
  orange rind
1 teaspoon salt
1½ tablespoons sugar
1 teaspoon paprika

Place all the ingredients in a saucepan, bring to the boil, then simmer for 15 minutes. Rub through a fine sieve to form a smooth sauce.

Serve hot or cold. Excellent served with scallops.

Makes 600 ml (1 pint)

BOLOGNAISE SAUCE

500 g (1 lb) minced
  beef
2 onions, chopped
2 cloves garlic,
  crushed
1 × 397 g (14 oz)
  can chopped
  tomatoes
1 × 65 g (2¼ oz)
  can tomato purée
2 teaspoons each dried
  basil and oregano
2 bay leaves
salt and pepper
TO SERVE:
1 tablespoon
  cornflour, blended
  with 2 tablespoons
  water

Put the beef in a large pan and cook over gentle heat, stirring, until browned. Add the onions and cook, stirring, until soft. Add the remaining ingredients, with salt and pepper to taste. Bring to the boil, cover and simmer for about 45 minutes, stirring occasionally.

Add the blended cornflour and simmer, stirring, for 2 to 3 minutes until thickened. Serve with pasta or use in recipes as stated.

Serves 4 to 6

Béchamel Sauce; Mayonnaise; Tuna Fish Mayonnaise; Piquant Green Sauce

TOMATO AND PRAWN SAUCE

25 g (1 oz) butter
1 onion, chopped
1 clove garlic, crushed
125 g (4 oz)
  mushrooms, sliced
500 g (1 lb)
  tomatoes, skinned
  and chopped
2 teaspoons tomato
  purée
½ teaspoon each
  dried basil and
  marjoram
3 tablespoons dry
  Vermouth
2 tablespoons lemon
  juice
salt and pepper
500 g (1 lb) peeled
  prawns
1 tablespoon cornflour
2 tablespoons oil
2 teaspoons cornflour,
  blended with 1
  tablespoon water

Melt the butter in a pan. Add the onion and garlic and cook until soft and transparent. Add the mushrooms and cook until soft, then stir in the tomatoes, tomato purée, herbs, Vermouth, lemon juice and a little salt and pepper.

Toss the prawns in the cornflour until evenly coated. Heat the oil in a pan, add the prawns and fry gently until golden. Stir into the sauce and simmer for about 5 minutes, stirring.

Stir in the blended cornflour and simmer, stirring, for 4 to 5 minutes. Check the seasoning and serve with pasta.

Serves 4 to 6

TOMATO AND PEPPER SAUCE

4 tablespoons oil
4 onions, chopped
2 large green peppers,
  cored, deseeded and
  chopped
2 × 397 g (14 oz)
  cans chopped
  tomatoes
salt and pepper
2 teaspoons
  Worcestershire
  sauce
1 bay leaf
1 tablespoon
  cornflour, blended
  with 2 tablespoons
  water (optional)

Heat the oil in a pan, add the onion and green pepper and fry until soft. Add the tomatoes with their juice, salt and pepper to taste, Worcestershire sauce and bay leaf. Simmer for about 30 minutes, until reduced to a thick pulp.

If a thick sauce is required, stir in the blended cornflour and bring to the boil; simmer, stirring, until thickened.

Serve with meat, fish or pasta.

Makes about 1.2 litres (2 pints)

CHICKEN LIVER SAUCE

50 g (2 oz) butter
1 small onion, chopped
50 g (2 oz) unsmoked streaky bacon, derinded and diced
50 g (2 oz) mushrooms, finely chopped
250 g (8 oz) chicken livers, diced
1 tablespoon plain flour
2 tablespoons Marsala
300 ml (½ pint) chicken stock
1 tablespoon tomato purée
salt and pepper

Melt 40 g (1½ oz) of the butter in a saucepan, add the onion and bacon and cook gently for 6 to 8 minutes, stirring occasionally. Increase the heat and add the mushrooms and chicken livers; cook, stirring, for 2 minutes. Add the flour and cook, stirring, for 1 minute.

Add the Marsala, bring to the boil, then stir in the stock, tomato purée and a little salt and pepper. Bring to the boil, cover and simmer for 30 to 40 minutes. Stir in the remaining butter and check the seasoning.

Serve hot with pasta or as required.
Serves 4

MEAT SAUCE

15 g (½ oz) butter
50 g (2 oz) smoked streaky bacon, derinded and diced
1 onion, chopped
1 small carrot, diced
1 celery stick, diced
375 g (12 oz) minced beef
2 tablespoons plain flour
450 ml (¾ pint) beef stock
1 tablespoon tomato purée
salt and pepper
grated nutmeg

Melt the butter in a pan, add the bacon, onion, carrot and celery and fry gently for 10 minutes, stirring frequently. Add the beef and cook, stirring, until browned. Stir in the flour and cook for 2 minutes.

Stir in the stock and tomato purée, and season with salt, pepper and nutmeg to taste. Bring to the boil, cover and simmer for 1 hour, stirring occasionally.

Serve with pasta.
Serves 4 to 6

Chicken Liver Sauce; Meat Sauce

RICH MEAT SAUCE

15 g (½ oz) butter
50 g (2 oz) smoked
    streaky bacon,
    derinded and diced
1 onion, finely
    chopped
1 small carrot,
    chopped
1 celery stick,
    chopped
375 g (12 oz) minced
    beef
125 g (4 oz) chicken
    livers, finely
    chopped
4 tablespoons dry
    Vermouth or white
    wine
300 ml (½ pint) beef
    stock
1 tablespoon tomato
    purée
salt and pepper
grated nutmeg
2 tablespoons single
    cream or top of the
    milk.

Melt the butter in a saucepan, add the bacon, onion, carrot and celery and fry gently for 10 minutes, stirring frequently. Add the beef and cook, stirring, until browned. Stir in the chicken livers and Vermouth or wine. Bring to the boil and cook until the liquid has almost completely evaporated.

Stir in the stock and tomato purée, and season with salt, pepper and nutmeg to taste. Bring back to the boil, cover and simmer for 1 hour, stirring occasionally. Check the seasoning and stir in the cream or milk.

Serve with tagliatelle, spaghetti or other pasta.
Serves 4 to 6

SPEEDY TOMATO SAUCE

1 × 400 g (14 oz)
    can peeled
    tomatoes
1 onion, chopped
1 clove garlic, crushed
1 carrot, sliced
1 celery stick, sliced
2 teaspoons tomato
    purée
1 teaspoon sugar
salt and pepper
2 teaspoons chopped
    basil (optional)

Put the tomatoes with their juice, the onion, garlic, carrot, celery, tomato purée and sugar into a saucepan. Add a little salt and pepper and stir with a wooden spoon to break up the tomatoes. Bring to the boil, partially cover and simmer for 30 minutes.

Rub through a sieve and return to the pan. If necessary, boil rapidly, uncovered, until reduced to a sauce consistency. Check the seasoning and stir in the basil, if using.

Serve as required, with pasta or meat dishes.
Makes about 300 ml (½ pint)

Rich Meat Sauce; Speedy Tomato Sauce; Tomato and Herb Sauce

TOMATO AND HERB SAUCE

2 tablespoons olive
    oil
2 cloves garlic,
    crushed
625 g (1¼ lb) ripe
    tomatoes, skinned
    and chopped
1 teaspoon sugar
salt and pepper
1 tablespoon chopped
    basil, oregano or
    parsley to garnish

Heat the oil and garlic gently in a saucepan for 2 minutes. Add the tomatoes, sugar, and salt and pepper to taste. Cook briskly for a few minutes until most of the liquid has evaporated and the tomatoes have softened but not reduced to a pulp.

Use as required with steaks, chops or fish. Garnish with herbs to serve.
Serves 4

INDEX